HARD YARDS

Gloucester Rugby
YEARBOOK
SEASON 2007 - 2008

Ed Snow

First published in 2008 by
HARD YARDS BOOKS

Photographs by
KEN DAVIS & BOB FENTON
unless otherwise credited

Statistics courtesy of
STUART FARMER; SFMS

ISBN 978 0 9559943 0 2

Typeset by
HARD YARDS BOOKS
GLOUCESTER; UK

HARD YARDS BOOKS

This book is dedicated to my sons Patrick and Peter who are both better players than I ever was – having represented Gloucester Colts and their respective universities - they are also better human beings than I could ever hope to be

AUTHOR'S PREFACE

Another season comes to an end and another edition of Hard Yards is published. I hope it brings as much joy to you reading and referring to it as writing it brought me.

I owe my thanks to a number of people who gave invaluable assistance in the preparation and production of this issue.
My wife June, for her unstinting support and reading and re-reading of drafts.
My sons Patrick and Peter for their continuing encouragement.
My friend Stuart Farmer of SFMS, for his assistance in compiling statistics.
Fellow Shedheads Ken Davis, who takes a serious rugby action photo and Bob Fenton, who is no mean performer with a camera himself.
Thank you – all of you – for your assistance and encouragement.

We are used to false dawns at Castle Grim. The road leading to this year is bestrewn with them but somehow you cannot help feeling that the winds of change – change for the better – are finally blowing across Kingsholm.
It is not unusual to feel like this at the start of a season but at the end of a long, hard season it is a new experience.

Just imagine how much more excited we are going to be at the end of the summer when the 2008 – 2009 season swings into action.

The depths of winter at Kingsholm has a peculiar charm of its own but for me, a sunny autumn afternoon is the best time to be alive and at Kingsholm. To stand in The Shed (alas, for me now that is mostly an experience from the past) with the late afternoon sun passing over the Grandstand and behind the cathedral is almost a spiritual experience.

That doyen of rugby writers, Stephen Jones of the Times, once said that if you could bottle the Kingsholm atmosphere you could sell it to other rugby clubs for a fortune. We are lucky, you and I. We do not need to buy a bottle of atmosphere; we contribute to the real thing. Just like Gloucester supporters before us have done, and those following us will surely do.

But as I write there is a lull in proceedings. It is currently the "off season", presumably so-called because it is the time of year that cheeses off all Shedheads and Shedettes.

We are going to have to fill our summer days the best way we can - cutting the grass, taking the kids on holiday, watching cricket.
All that normal sort of stuff until the mornings once again have that certain chill in the air; that overwhelming feeling of anticipation, and we find ourselves looking forward to the first home game of the season.

If you see me at Kingsholm and you have some constructive criticism, come up and have a chat; I will look forward to it. Who knows, your suggestions could appear in next season's Hard Yards.

Ed Smith

CONTENTS

An Overview...

The season started with five Guinness Premiership wins on the bounce. In this sequence: away, away, home, away, home, taking us through to the tail end of October.

Then a Guinness Premiership loss to London Irish at the Madejski Stadium presaged a couple of bad results for us: an eighteen-all draw with Newcastle at Kingsholm in the EDF Cup, followed by a loss to Wasps at Adams Park. Taken in isolation these three results do not look too bad, but at the time, coming one after another following a five-match winning sequence, they struck the average Gloucester supporter as dire.

However, as November continued we strung together an impressive eight wins back-to-back which took us through to the start of January. Our victories included two away wins in the Heineken Cup at Ravenhill and Stade Pierre Rajon; two home wins in the Heineken Cup against Ospreys and Bourgoin and an EDF Cup victory at Rodney Parade for good measure. We also managed three Guinness Premiership wins against Harlequins at Kingsholm, Newcastle Falcons away and a twenty seven points to nil whitewashing of Bristol at Kingsholm.

So, with only one draw and two losses blotting our copybook from the first sixteen matches of the season we went down to the Rec on the banks of the River Avon to confront Bath in our latest attempt to end our Premiership jinx. It was our first match of the new year and so waterlogged was the pitch it might just as well have been played in the Avon as upon its banks, Irrespective of the difficulties getting to the Friday night match the travelling Gloucester support was immense, although an all-pervading feeling of pessimism was growing by the minute. They crossed their fingers and hoped for a postponement. Surely Dean Ryan did as well but referee Wayne Barnes deemed it playable so we played and we lost on a pitch that was too wet even for water polo! In reasonable conditions we would have annihilated them so, a referee's absurd decision probably cost us a win. Nothing new there, then...

Eight days later we lost to the Ospreys in the Heineken Cup at the Liberty Stadium and our season started to take on a familiar kind of feel. A good start, then a few faltering steps as we tried to get back on course. A pretty forgettable middle to the season and then – we hoped – a grandstand finish.

We won two more matches which brought us to the end of January and as February started we lost at Kingsholm to Leicester which we quickly followed with an away loss to Bristol Rugby at the Memorial Ground. Another Guinness Premiership win and then another loss, this time it was against Harlequins at The Stoop. Our traditional mid-season floundering seemed to be hanging on into the sharp end of the season.

One more win and then a string of three losses – two Guinness Premiership away matches and then the Heineken Cup quarter final at Kingsholm - took us through to April when we strung together four back-to-back Guinness Premiership matches. Ending with a Kingsholm victory over Bath.

Our last match of the season was the Guinness Premiership Championship semi final against Leicester.

With Bath playing Wasps in the other semi final we started to see an avenue for revenge for our humiliation at Twickenham in the 1990 cup final when Bath stuck 48 points on us against only six of our own. If Bath beat Wasps that would put them in the final on a June day when the advantage would be in our favour.

So fervently did we hope for a Wasps loss against Bath that we failed to notice the ambush cunningly set for us by Leicester and neither of us got to Twickenham.

There were some notable occurrences on our journey through the season. Some of our new players made names for themselves and some of our established players disappeared off the radar through injury or lack of form.

Qera and Strokosch were revelations. Far from being makeweights they turned out to be the stars of the season, particularly Qera whose speed and tackling ability made life difficult for Andy Hazell to impose himself on our season to the extent he would have liked. Qera was in the running for *Guinness Premiership Player of the Season Award* and Strokosch was awarded the *Guinness Premiership Player of the Month Award* in December.

Mike Tindall got himself injured again. This time with an accidental kick during the England-Wales Six Nations match at

Twickenham when a freak accident caused him serious problems.

He thought at first he had only winded himself, but the searing pain did not stop. It was quelled by morphine and he eventually finished up in intensive care at Hammersmith Hospital where surgeons diagnosed that a hole had been torn in his liver and he had punctured lung, just for good measure.

On the subject of injuries, James 'Django' Forrester continues to show good spirits despite his prolonged lay-off. Although no longer in the England Elite Player Squad it will not be long before he forces himself back into contention.

Meanwhile, Luke Narraway forges ahead with his international career and inclusion in the England Elite Players Squad.

Three Academy players Norton, Sharples and Trinder made their first team debuts – returning from Moseley where they had been on loan under the watchful eye of ex-Gloucester stalwart and now Moseley coach, Ian Smith. Adam Balding, who was also on loan, this time to Leeds Carnegie, was also recalled for cover of frontline duties.

World Cup points-kicking record holder Chris Paterson decided to call it a day in this neck of the woods, even though he put in several good performances, including scoring all our points against Bath at the Recreation Ground. It is widely believed that his departure was hastened by despair at unsigned and largely unwarranted sniping on unofficial Gloucester rugby websites.

Two fine campaigners for France's cause called it a day at Kingsholm at the end of the season when props Christian Califano and Patrice Collazo hung up their boots for the last time. This period was Collazo's second sojourn at the club.

His final match was played at Kingsholm as a Barbarian against Ireland on 27 May 2008, alongside Gloucester Rugby club mate Lesley Vainikolo. Meanwhile, we learn that Cali intends to take a long holiday before returning to rugby – in France or England – in a coaching capacity in a season or two. As we go to press, reports are being received that he is standing for the Socialist Party in local elections in the Mid-Pyrenees region.

As we go to print we at Hard Yards are unsure whether we wave goodbye to Willie Walker or not. Official reports say he is to join the ever-lengthening list of Kingsholm favourites making their way up the M5 to Sixways.

Whereas as yet unconfirmed reports say his skills, experience and sense of humour will be too hard to replace and he is to renew his Kingsholm contract. Fingers crossed on that one...

Player selection, as always, has been a hot talking point. For example, it was difficult to comprehend how Gareth Cooper could be selected to tour South Africa with Wales; yet he was not considered first choice scrum half for Gloucester.

Then there is the mystery of the disappearing Karl Pryce. Along with Big Lesley Vainikolo he was recruited to put some more muscle in our backline following its exposure by the Leicester backs at Twickenham in the 2006 - 2007 Premiership Championship. Pryce made his debut in the Newcastle Falcons match at Kingsholm in the EDF Cup (although he was in the Gloucester squad at the 2007 Middlesex Sevens).

He looked incapable of deciding whether he should be going forwards to support an attack, or retreating to offer defensive cover. He did handle the ball once or twice and also got involved in a ruck or two where he may have picked up an injury. After a very uncomfortable-looking half hour or so
he was replaced by James Bailey and never seen in action again.

The official version is his contract was terminated by mutual consent but he did look very ponderous in his debut match and it is widely believed that he suffered a renewed fracture of a bone in his left foot - an injury he originally sustained playing rugby league at Bradford Bulls. Since leaving Kingsholm he has signed for Wigan Warriors Rugby League Club.

That is the second time Gloucester has signed a rugby league player who, despite showing all the promise in the world, failed to live up to expectations on the pitch. Henry Paul was the first and although he sometimes displayed his unquestioned genius on the pitch, he tended to blow hot and cold. Unfortunately for Gloucester he tended to blow more cold than hot while at Kingsholm.

So, now we have Big Les, signed from Bradford Bulls and he seems to be ticking a lot of boxes, having played for England and the Barbarians in the same season. Unlike Pryce, he burst onto the Premiership stage with all the razzmatazz of a burlesque stripper bursting out of a cardboard cake, scoring a personal tally of five tries in his first ever rugby union match, away at Leeds Headingley.

From there he went from strength to strength and his meteoric rise in rugby union was reinforced by his selection for England's Six Nations squad by Brian Ashton and his season culminated in donning a Barbarians jersey at Kingsholm.

Big Les' Six Nations campaign was not quite such a dramatic event as his Gloucester matches. A fact which was largely due to the churlishness of his England team mates who steadfastly refused to pass him the ball.
Reading between the lines there seemed to be a resentment of him within the England team. He was a convert from rugby league who had only played a handful of rugby union matches and he was a native of the southern hemisphere who only qualified for England by reason of residency. There were strong inferences that he was resented under both these heads which resulted in him being starved of possession. So he stood out on the wing like a spare part and England lost to Wales by 19 points to 26. He did manage to show his capabilities though, when he gathered a cross kick and passed to Flood who scored. Had his England "team mates" used him properly they could probably have won the match.
Later on in the campaign; in the Ireland match, Les' red dreadlocks were so arranged as to spell out "Raging Bull". A masterpiece of marketing by somebody – probably ex-Gloucester and England captain PJ Vickery MBE.

There is just one slight niggle at the back of Hard Yards' mind, though. Big Les was brought in to put some steel into our backline following their decimation by Leicester at Twickenham last season. In the semi final of the Premiership Championship this season Big Les came face to face with our nemesis: Alesana Tuilagi.
Big Les' body positioning was less than perfect and he got knocked fairly and squarely onto his backside while Tuilagi went on to score a try.
So, although with ball in hand Big Lesley Vainikolo is devastating there is just the merest hint of a question mark

about his rugby union defensive qualities; or perhaps Hard Yards is being too picky.

Hard Yards' high spot of the season was beating Bath at Kingsholm. That is always a very special occasion and it cemented our place at the top of the league so it was doubly enjoyable.

It goes without saying that the low spot came right on the very last day of our season when we got ourselves ambushed by a Leicester team which could not quite believe its luck in being in the Premiership play-offs. Even their coach, Richard Cockerill was on record the week before saying that his charges would not get into the play-offs and even if they did, they would not win the final because they were not good enough.

It seemed that the Gloucester Rugby team believed Cockerill's disloyalty and thought all they needed to do was turn up to get into the final. We wish...

James Simpson-Daniel was voted the *Shedhead Reader's Player of the Season* and on 28 May 2008 he added the Guinness Premiership Player of the Season Award, presented by Land Rover. Sinbad has been a key figure in the Gloucester squad since making his debut in 2000. He has played over 100 Premiership matches and scored 41 tries for Gloucester.

Sinbad was clearly the best-performing Gloucester Rugby player this season. Accumulating 10 tries; making 26 breaks; making 16 offloads; beating 32 defenders and carrying for Gloucester's second-highest total of 942 metres, a mere 4 metres behind Big Les' total of 942 metres.

So, Gloucester Rugby had to wait for the appointment of Martin Johnson before the best statistical performer in the top league club was awarded his rightful place in the England Elite Player Squad.

Until Jonno's appearance on the scene James Simpson-Daniel had been largely ignored by the RFU for international honours. How does that work?

This season he achieved his best league haul ever with 10 tries from 18 Guinness Premiership appearances; including a couple of *Try of the Season* contenders – one in Round 22 against Bath and the other in the Premiership Championship play-off semi final against Leicester Tigers. His try against Bath was voted second best try of the season, being narrowly pipped by Worcester's length-of-the-pitch effort.

It was his try against Leicester that confirmed him as Gloucester Rugby's top try scorer in the 2007 - 2008 season and the second highest scorer in the league behind Leicester Tigers' Tom Varndell who claimed the Coral Top Try Scorer of the Season award for the second time in three seasons.

A shoulder injury kept him out of England's summer tests but there is no reason why he should not force his way into contention for the November tests with a real chance to increase his current England caps tally of 10.

In second place behind Sinbad was Bath's Olly Barkley who made a huge contribution to his club finishing third in the Premiership and winning the European Challenge Cup. He showed such good form during the season that he could not be ignored for this summer's New Zealand tour. A point which bodes well for the new season when he makes the 40-mile trip from the Rec to Kingsholm to play his rugby.

Then in third place behind Sinbad and Barkley was Akapusi Qera. In his first season our Fijian flanker took the Premiership by storm. Impressing all and sundry with his pace, power and physicality in attack and defence.

The title of *O2 Director of Rugby of the Season* was awarded to Gloucester Rugby's Dean Ryan. Why not? We were top of the Premiership table for 21 of the 22 rounds and finished the season as the league's second highest try scorers. We reached the quarter final of the European Cup, losing to the eventual winners, Munster.
Dean has centred his team around a core of young talent but has not been afraid to strengthen his squad with signings which bring experience and alternative talents to the squad.

So, although we stumbled at the final hurdle, which left a painful wound, once that raw stabbing pain of loss had subsided to a dull ache and we were able to look at the season with a more dispassionate eye, we could see that it had been a good, solid, successful season. For the club; for the team; for individual players and managers and for us supporters, too.

Results

GUINNESS PREMIERSHIP

Date	Kickoff	Opponents	H/A	Score	W/D/L
Sunday 16 September	3.00pm	Leeds Carnegie	A	24 - 29	W
Sunday 23 September	3.00pm	Saracens	A	31 - 38	W
Saturday 29 September	6.00pm	Worcester Warriors	H	29 - 7	W
Saturday 6 October	6.00pm	Leicester Tigers	A	17 - 30	W
Saturday 13 October	3.00pm	Sale Sharks	H	31 - 12	W
Sunday 21 October	4.00pm	London Irish	A	15 - 10	L
Saturday 24 November	3.00pm	Harlequins	H	27 - 25	W
Sunday 23 December	3.00pm	Newcastle Falcons	A	13 - 20	W
Saturday 29 December	3.00pm	Bristol Rugby	H	27 - 0	W
Friday 4 January	8.00pm	Bath Rugby	A	10 - 5	L
Saturday 26 January	3.00pm	London Wasps	H	18 - 17	W
Saturday 9 February	3.00pm	Leicester Tigers	A	13 - 20	L
Sunday 17 February	3.00pm	Bristol Rugby	A	29 - 26	L
Saturday 23 February	3.00pm	Newcastle Falcons	H	28 - 20	W
Saturday 1 March	2.45pm	Harlequins	A	30 - 25	L
Saturday 8 March	5.30pm	London Irish	H	34 - 14	W
Friday 14 March	7.45pm	Sale Sharks	A	22 - 16	L
Saturday 29 March	3.00pm	Worcester Warriors	A	17 - 14	L
Saturday 12 April	12.35pm	Saracens	H	39 - 15	W
Saturday 19 April	3.00pm	Leeds Carnegie	H	39 - 16	W
Sunday 4 May	3.00pm	London Wasps	A	17 - 25	W
Saturday 10 May	3.00pm	Bath Rugby	H	8 - 6	W
* Sunday 18 May	4.30pm	Leicester Tigers	H	25 – 26	L

* Guinness Premiership Championship semi final

HEINEKEN CUP

Date	Kickoff	Opponents	H/A	Score	W/D/L
Friday 9 November	8.00pm	Ulster	A	14 - 32	W
Friday 16 November	8.00pm	Ospreys	H	26 - 18	W
Friday 7 December	9.00pm	Bourgoin	A	7 - 31	W
Saturday 15 December	3.00pm	Bourgoin	H	51 - 27	W
Saturday 12 January	5.30pm	Ospreys	A	32 - 15	L
Sunday 20 January	1.00pm	Ulster	H	29 - 21	W
* Saturday 5 April	5.30pm	Munster	H	3 - 16	L

* Heineken Cup quarter final

EDF CUP

Date	Kickoff	Opponents	H/A	Score	W/D/L
Saturday 27 October	3.00pm	Newcastle Falcons	H	18 - 18	D
Sunday 4 November	3.00pm	London Wasps	A	29 - 26	L
Friday 30 November	7.30pm	Dragons	A	11 - 13	W

Players Leaving

Jake Boer Retired

Brad Davies Joined Plymouth Albion RFC

Mefin Davies Joined Leicester Tigers

Rob Elloway Joined Cornish Pirates RFC

Adam Eustace Joined Llanelli Scarlets

Jon Goodridge Joined Leeds Carnegie

Rudi Keil Joined Sale Sharks

James Merriman Joined Neath RFC

Ludovic Mercier

Dean Miller

Peter Richards Joined London Irish RFC

Terry Sigley Joined Moseley RFC

Rob Thirlby Joined Redruth RFC

Haydn Thomas Joined Bristol Rugby

Players Joining

Gareth Cooper Signed from Gwent Dragons

Alasdair Dickinson Signed from Edinburgh Gunners

Gareth Delve Signed from Bath Rugby

Ali James Signed from Newbury RFC

Dave Lewis

Leon Lloyd Signed from Leicester Tigers

Akapusi Qera Signed from Pertemps Bees

Chris Paterson Signed from Edinburgh Gunners

Jeremy Paul Signed from ACT Brumbies

Mike Prendergast Signed from Bourgoin

Karl Pryce Signed from Wigan RL

Alasdair Strokosch Signed from Edinburgh Gunners

Andy Titterrell Signed from Sale Sharks

Lesley Vainikolo Signed from Bradford Bulls

2007 – 2008 SQUAD

Jack Adams	Jack Forster	Chris Paterson
Anthony Allen	Mark Foster	Jeremy Paul
Olivier Azam	Andy Hazell	Jonathan Pendlebury
James Bailey	Ali James	Mike Prendergast
Adam Balding	Will James	Karl Pryce
Iain Balshaw	Ryan Lamb	James Simpson-Daniel
Marco Bortolami	Rory Lawson	Charlie Sharples
Alex Brown	Dave Lewis	Alasdair Strokosch
Peter Buxton	Leon Lloyd	Mike Tindall
Christian Califano	Ross McMillan	Andy Titterrell
Patrice Collazo	Olly Morgan	Henry Trinder
Gareth Cooper	Luke Narraway	Dan Tuohy
Gareth Delve	Carlos Nieto	Lesley Vainikolo
Alasdair Dickinson	Dan Norton	Willie Walker
James Forrester	Akapusi Qera	Nick Wood

GUINNESS PREMIERSHIP
Gloucester Rugby - top performers

Ball Carries

L Narraway	145
A Allen	130
A Strokosch	98

Tackles

A Strokosch	191
P Buxton	184
L Narraway	178

Metres Gained

L Vainikolo	946
J S-Daniel	942
A Allen	724

Lineouts Won

A Brown	61
M Bortolami	46
L Narraway	29

Defenders Beaten

A Allen	44
J S-Daniel	32
L Vainikolo	29

Tries

J S-Daniel	10
L Vainikolo	9
O Azam	5

Breaks Made

J S-Daniel	26
A Allen	14
L Vainikolo	14

Points

R Lamb	169
W Walker	80
J S-Daniel	50

Offloads

J S-Daniel	16
A Allen	12
L Vainikolo	11

Yellow Cards

M Bortolami	3
R Lamb	2
W James	2

GUINNESS PREMIERSHIP
Top Performers – Comparative Charts

DEFENDERS BEATEN
1 Sailosi Tagicakibau   68
2 Tom Guest   50
3 Matt Banahan   49
4 Mike Brown   45
5= Anthony Allen   **43**
5= Ben Foden   43
5= Oriol Ripol Fortuny   43
8 Riki Flutey   41
9= Olly Barkley   38
9= Sam Tuitupou   38
9= John Rudd   38

BREAKS MADE
1 Sailosi Tagicakibau   24
1 James S-Daniel   **24**
3= Matt Banahan   23
3= Kameli Ratuvou   23
5 Adam Powell   21
6= Josh Lewsey   20
6= Ben Foden   20
8= Tom Arscott   19
8= Paul Sackey   19
8= Johne Murphy   19

TACKLES MADE
1 Chris Robshaw   223
2 James Haskel   198
3 Alasdair Strokosch   **195**
4 Pat Sanderson   191
5 Will Skinner   186
6 Peter Buxton   **184**
7 Matt Salter   181
8 Riki Flutey   180
9 Luke Narraway   **176**
10 Anthony Allen   **164**

TACKLES MISSED
1 Alberto di Bernardo   29
2 James Haskell   26
3= Anthony Allen   **25**
3= Charlie Hodgson   25
5= Joe Bedford   24
5= Leigh Hinton   24
5= Ryan Lamb   **24**
8= Adrian Jarvis   23
8= Sam Tuitupou   23
8= Danny Cipriani   23

OWN LINEOUT WON
1 Nick Kennedy   88
2 Craig Gillies   79
3= Sean Hohneck   72
3= Geoff Parling   72
5 Mark Sorenson   71
6 Ben Skirving   69
7 Tom Palmer   65
8 Alex Brown   **62**
9 Bob Casey   61
10 George Skivington   59

LINEOUT STEALS
1 Craig Gillies   21
2 Nick Kennedy   16
3 Bob Casey   14
4= Mark Sorenson   12
4= Tom Croft   12
4= Chris Jones   12
7 Nicolas Spanghero   10
8= Alex Brown   **8**
8= Louis Deacon   8
8= Drew Hickey   8
8= Marco Wentzel   8

TRIES

1	Tom Varndell	14
2=	Matt Banahan	10
2=	**James S-Daniel**	**10**
4=	Miles Benjamin	9
4=	**Lesley Vainikolo**	**9**
6=	Ben Foden	8
6=	Tom Voyce	8
8=	Tom May	7
8=	Paul Sackey	7
8=	Tom Biggs	7

TRY ASSISTS

1	Danny Cipriani	11
2	Shane Drahm	10
3	Chris Malone	7
4=	Shaun Berne	6
4=	Adam Powell	6
4=	Charlie Hodgson	6
4=	Andy Goode	6
8=	**Ryan Lamb**	**5**
8=	Glen Jackson	5
8=	Riki Flutey	5
8=	D Lemi	5

CONVERSIONS

1	Danny Cipriani	39
2	Olly Barkley	31
3	Glen Jackson	29
4	Andy Goode	26
5	**Ryan Lamb**	**25**
6	Charlie Hodgson	22
7	Chris Malone	20
8	Shane Drahm	19
9	Adrian Jarvis	17
10	Alberto di Bernardo	14

CONVERSION MISSED

1	**Ryan Lamb**	**16**
2=	Andy Goode	15
2=	Shane Drahm	15
4	Glen Jackson	14

5	Peter Hewat	10
6	Chris Malone	9
7	Danny Cipriani	8
8=	Adrian Jarvis	7
8=	Olly Barkley	7
8=	Shaun Berne	7
8=	Ed Barnes	7

PENALTY GOALS

1	Andy Goode	46
2	Charlie Hodgson	41
3	Glen Jackson	35
4=	Olly Barkley	32
4=	**Ryan Lamb**	**32**
6=	Alberto Di Bernardo	28
6=	Danny Cipriani	28
8	Adrian Jarvis	27
9	Shane Drahm	24
10	Jason Strange	22

MISSED PENALTY GOALS

1	Andy Goode	28
2=	Danny Cipriani	16
2=	Chris Malone	16
4=	Adrian Jarvis	13
4=	Glen Jackson	13
6	**Ryan Lamb**	**12**
7=	Shane Drahm	11
7=	Charlie Hodgson	11
7=	Alberto di Bernardo	11
10=	Jonny Wilkinson	10
10=	Peter Hewat	10

DROPPED GOALS

1	Charlie Hodgson	9
2	Alberto Di Bernardo	5
3	Andy Goode	4
4=	Chris Malone	2
4=	Glen Jackson	2
4=	Dave Walder	2
4=	Tom May	2
8=	Riki Flutey	1

8= Ryan Lamb	**1**
8= Gordon Ross	1

POINTS

1 Andy Goode	207
2 Charlie Hodgson	104
3 Danny Cipriani	192
4 Glen Jackson	179
5 Olly Barkley	173
6 Ryan Lamb	**169**
7 Alberto di Bernardo	127
8 Shane Drahm	118
9 Adrian Jarvis	115
10 Chris Malone	107

KICKS FROM HAND

1 Charlie Hodgson	293
2 Andy Goode	224
3 Ryan Lamb	**195**
4 A di Bernardo	192
5 Shane Drahm	159
6 Glen Jackson	154
7 Chris Malone	140

8 Danny Cipriani	131
9 Peter Hewat	129
10 Willie Walker	**125**

YELLOW CARDS

1= Marco Bortolami	**3**
1= Stuart Hooper	3
1= Tom Wood	3
4= Delon Armitage	2
4= James Haskell	2
4= Ryan Lamb	**2**
4= Michael Claassens	2
4= Jordan Crane	2
4= Will James	**2**
4= Viliami Ma'asi	2

RED CARDS

Ben Herring	1
de Wet Barry	1

GUINNESS PREMIERSHIP
Team Performance – Comparative Charts

DEFENDERS BEATEN
1	Bath Rugby	351
2	London Wasps	327
3	Leicester Tigers	305
4	Sale Sharks	304
5	Saracens	283
6	Bristol Rugby	281
7	Harlequins	280
8	**Gloucester Rugby**	**279**
9	London Irish	252
9	Worcester Warriors	252
11	Newcastle Falcons	230
12	Leeds Carnegie	206

BREAKS MADE
1	London Wasps	196
2	Saracens	184
3	Bath Rugby	183
4	Leicester Tigers	156
5	**Gloucester Rugby**	**148**
6	Sale Sharks	132
7	London Irish	131
8	Bristol Rugby	129
9	Worcester Warriors	124
10	Harlequins	121
11	Newcastle Falcons	117
12	Leeds Carnegie	95

TACKLES MADE
1	London Wasps	2944
2	**Gloucester Rugby**	**2756**
3	Leeds Carnegie	2724
4	Leicester Tigers	2443
5	Saracens	2396
6	Harlequins	2347
7	Newcastle Falcons	2299
8	Bristol Rugby	2293
9	Bath Rugby	2216
10	Sale Sharks	2181
11	Worcester Warriors	2126
12	London Irish	2097

TACKLES MISSED
1	Leeds Carnegie	348
2	London Wasps	321
3	Newcastle Falcons	308
4	Leicester Tigers	300
4	Saracens	300
6	Harlequins	277
7	London Irish	276
8	**Gloucester Rugby**	**274**
9	Bristol Rugby	271
10	Sale Sharks	253
11	Worcester Warriors	222
12	Bath Rugby	194

LINEOUTS WON
1	Sale Sharks	296
2	London Wasps	280
3	Newcastle Falcons	275
4	Leicester Tigers	271
5	London Irish	268
6	**Gloucester Rugby**	**266**
7	Bristol Rugby	265
8	Harlequins	262
9	Bath Rugby	258
10	Saracens	252
11	Leeds Carnegie	250
12	Worcester Warriors	247

LINEOUTS LOST
1	Bristol Rugby	78
2	Sale Sharks	77
3	Newcastle Falcons	67
3	**Gloucester Rugby**	**67**
5	Leeds Carnegie	64
6	Saracens	57

7 Harlequins	53
8 Worcester Warriors	52
9 Bath Rugby	49
10 Leicester Tigers	46
11 London Wasps	45
12 London Irish	29

7 Gloucester Rugby	209
7 Bath Rugby	209
9 Saracens	202
10 Bristol Rugby	201
11 Sale Sharks	196
12 London Irish	188

SCRUMS WON

1 Leicester Tigers	214
1 London Wasps	214
3 Worcester Warriors	199
4 Bath Rugby	198
4 Gloucester Rugby	**198**
4 Harlequins	198
7 Leeds Carnegie	197
8 Newcastle Falcons	190
9 Sale Sharks	183
10 Bristol Rugby	181
10 Saracens	181
12 London Irish	165

RUCKS WON

1 Bath Rugby	2055
2 London Wasps	1897
3 Leicester Tigers	1706
4 Bristol Rugby	1676
5 Newcastle Falcons	1675
6 Saracens	1638
7 London Irish	1568
8 Sale Sharks	1559
9 Worcester Warriors	1506
10 Harlequins	1490
11 Leeds Carnegie	1486
12 Gloucester Rugby	**1407**

SCRUMS LOST

1 London Wasps	26
1 Leeds Carnegie	26
3 London Irish	23
4 Saracens	21
5 Newcastle Falcons	20
5 Bristol Rugby	20
7 Worcester Warriors	18
8 Leicester Tigers	17
9 Sale Sharks	13
9 Harlequins	13
11 Gloucester Rugby	**11**
11 Bath Rugby	11

RUCKS LOST

1 Bath Rugby	94
2 London Wasps	82
2 London Irish	82
4 Newcastle Falcons	78
5 Saracens	77
6 Worcester Warriors	74
7 Leeds Carnegie	71
8 Harlequins	70
8 Leicester Tigers	70
10 Bristol Rugby	69
11 Gloucester Rugby	**68**
12 Sale Sharks	63

SCRUMS TOTAL

1 London Wasps	240
2 Leicester Tigers	231
3 Leeds Carnegie	223
4 Worcester Warriors	217
5 Harlequins	211
6 Newcastle Falcons	210

RUCKS TOTAL

1 Bath Rugby	2149
2 London Wasps	1979
3 Leicester Tigers	1776
4 Newcastle Falcons	1753
5 Bristol Rugby	1745
6 Saracens	1715

7	London Irish	1650
8	Sale Sharks	1622
9	Worcester Warriors	1580
10	Harlequins	1560
11	Leeds Carnegie	1557
12	**Gloucester Rugby**	**1475**

TOTAL TRIES

1	London Wasps	72
2	**Gloucester Rugby**	**66**
3	Leicester Tigers	62
4	Bath Rugby	60
5	Saracens	58
6	Harlequins	53
7	Worcester Warriors	48
8	Sale Sharks	44
8	London Irish	44
10	Bristol Rugby	40
11	Newcastle Falcons	34
12	Leeds Carnegie	33

PASSES

1	Bath Rugby	3059
2	Saracens	2866
3	London Wasps	2516
4	Newcastle Falcons	2467
5	Leicester Tigers	2465
6	London Irish	2446
7	Worcester Warriors	2360
8	Bristol Rugby	2352
9	Sale Sharks	2325
10	**Gloucester Rugby**	**2107**
11	Harlequins	1923
12	Leeds Carnegie	1849

KICKS FROM HAND

1	Sale Sharks	661
2	**Gloucester Rugby**	**630**
3	Harlequins	598
4	London Irish	595
5	Leeds Carnegie	582
6	Leicester Tigers	573

7	Worcester Warriors	543
8	Bath Rugby	528
9	Newcastle Falcons	508
10	Saracens	484
11	London Wasps	480
12	Bristol Rugby	469

BALL CARRIES

1	Bath Rugby	2507
2	London Wasps	2426
3	Leicester Tigers	2147
4	Bristol Rugby	2137
5	Saracens	2054
6	Newcastle Falcons	1962
7	London Irish	1950
8	Sale Sharks	1923
9	Worcester Warriors	1865
10	Leeds Carnegie	1837
11	Harlequins	1799
12	**Gloucester Rugby**	**1738**

METRES MADE

1	Bath Rugby	11132
2	London Wasps	10718
3	Saracens	10032
4	Leicester Tigers	9741
5	London Irish	8952
6	**Gloucester Rugby**	**8514**
7	Worcester Warriors	8391
8	Sale Sharks	8390
9	Bristol Rugby	8187
10	Newcastle Falcons	7881
11	Harlequins	7584
12	Leeds Carnegie	7335

CONVERSION GOALS

1	London Wasps	59
2	Bath Rugby	43
3	**Gloucester Rugby**	**42**
4	Saracens	39
5	Leicester Tigers	38
6	Harlequins	37

7 Sale Sharks	33	7 Worcester Warriors	167
8 Worcester Warriors	27	8 Sale Sharks	165
9 Bristol Rugby	26	9 Leeds Carnegie	155
10 Leeds Carnegie	21	10 Harlequins	154
11 Newcastle Falcons	20	11 Newcastle Falcons	139
12 London Irish	18	**12 Gloucester Rugby**	**130**

DROPPED GOALS

1 Sale Sharks	9
2 Newcastle Falcons	6
2 Leicester Tigers	6
4 Leeds Carnegie	5
5 Saracens	3
5 London Wasps	3
5 Harlequins	3
8 Gloucester Rugby	**2**
8 London Irish	2
8 Worcester Warriors	2
11 Bristol Rugby	1
11 Bath Rugby	1

YELLOW CARDS

1 London Wasps	12
1 Worcester Warriors	12
3 Gloucester Rugby	**11**
3 Leeds Carnegie	11
3 London Irish	11
6 Leicester Tigers	9
6 Harlequins	9
8 Newcastle Falcons	8
8 Sale Sharks	8
10 Saracens	7
10 Bath Rugby	7
12 Bristol Rugby	6

OFFLOADS

1 Bath Rugby	214
2 Leicester Tigers	205
3 Bristol Rugby	194
4 London Wasps	187
5 London Irish	176
6 Saracens	175

RED CARDS

1 Leicester Tigers	1
1 Harlequins	1

2007 – 2008 GLOUCESTER RUGBY
TEAM PERFORMANCE

PREMIERSHIP		HEINEKEN CUP		EDFE CUP	
Start	345	Start	105	Start	45
Replacement	116	Replacement	42	Replacement	18
Sub not used	45	Sub not used	7	Sub not used	3
Replaced	135	Replaced	46	Replaced	19
Penalty Try	2	Penalty Try	0	Penalty Try	0
Try	66	Try	42	Try	7
Conversion	42	Conversion	17	Conversion	5
Penalty goal	52	Penalty goal	11	Penalty goal	0
Drop goal	2	Drop goal	0	Drop goal	4
Total points	576	Total points	187	Total points	57
Red card	0	Red card	0	Red card	0
Yellow card	6	Yellow card	6	Yellow card	0

27490 minutes in play   8353 minutes in play   3590 minutes in play

INDIVIDUAL PERFORMANCES
Jack Adams

PREMIERSHIP

Start	5
Replacement	1
Sub not used	1
Replaced	4
Try	3
Conversion	0
Penalty goal	0
Drop goal	0
Total points	15
Red card	0
Yellow card	0
Won	3
Drew	0
Lost	3

328 minutes in play

Anthony Allen

PREMIERSHIP		HEINEKEN CUP		EDFE CUP	
Start	20	Start	7	Start	2
Replacement	1	Replacement	0	Replacement	0
Sub not used	0	Sub not used	0	Sub not used	0
Replaced	2	Replaced	2	Replaced	0
Try	4	Try	2	Try	0
Conversion	0	Conversion	0	Conversion	0
Penalty goal	0	Penalty goal	0	Penalty goal	0
Drop goal	0	Drop goal	0	Drop goal	0
Total points	20	Total points	10	Total points	0
Red card	0	Red card	0	Red card	0
Yellow card	0	Yellow card	0	Yellow card	0
Won	13	Won	5	Won	0
Drew	0	Drew	0	Drew	1
Lost	8	Lost	2	Lost	1
1582 minutes in play		516 minutes in play		160 minutes in play	

Olivier Azam

PREMIERSHIP		HEINEKEN CUP		EDFE CUP	
Start	10	Start	5	Start	1
Replacement	10	Replacement	1	Replacement	0
Sub not used	0	Sub not used	0	Sub not used	0
Replaced	11	Replaced	5	Replaced	1
Try	5	Try	0	Try	1
Conversion	0	Conversion	0	Conversion	0
Penalty goal	0	Penalty goal	0	Penalty goal	0
Drop goal	0	Drop goal	0	Drop goal	0
Total points	25	Total points	0	Total points	5
Red card	0	Red card	0	Red card	0
Yellow card	1	Yellow card	1	Yellow card	0
Won	15	Won	5	Won	0
Drew	0	Drew	0	Drew	0
Lost	5	Lost	2	Lost	1
841 minutes in play		318 min in play		52 minutes in play	

James Bailey

PREMIERSHIP		EDFE CUP	
Start	9	Start	1
Replacement	1	Replacement	1
Sub not used	0	Sub not used	0
Replaced	2	Replaced	0
Try	5	Try	0
Conversion	0	Conversion	0
Penalty goal	0	Penalty goal	0
Drop goal	0	Drop goal	0
Total points	25	Total points	0
Red card	0	Red card	0
Yellow card	1	Yellow card	0
Won	15	Won	1
Drew	0	Drew	1
Lost	5	Lost	0

719 minutes in play   130 minutes in play

Adam Balding

PREMIERSHIP		EDFE CUP	
Start	1	Start	1
Replacement	1	Replacement	0
Sub not used	1	Sub not used	0
Replaced	1	Replaced	0
Try	0	Try	0
Conversion	0	Conversion	0
Penalty goal	0	Penalty goal	0
Drop goal	0	Drop goal	0
Total points	0	Total points	0
Red card	0	Red card	0
Yellow card	0	Yellow card	0
Won	1	Won	0
Drew	0	Drew	1
Lost	1	Lost	0

73 Minutes in play   80 minutes in play

Iain Balshaw

PREMIERSHIP		HEINEKEN CUP		EDFE CUP	
Start	13	Start	6	Start	2
Replacement	1	Replacement	0	Replacement	0
Sub not used	1	Sub not used	0	Sub not used	0
Replaced	2	Replaced	2	Replaced	0
Try	4	Try	3	Try	1
Conversion	0	Conversion	0	Conversion	0
Penalty goal	0	Penalty goal	0	Penalty goal	0
Drop goal	0	Drop goal	0	Drop goal	0
Total points	20	Total points	15	Total points	5
Red card	0	Red card	0	Red card	0
Yellow card	0	Yellow card	0	Yellow card	0
Won	9	Won	5	Won	0
Drew	0	Drew	0	Drew	1
Lost	5	Lost	1	Lost	1

1015 minutes in play   436 minutes in play   160 minutes in play

Marco Bortolami

PREMIERSHIP		HEINEKEN CUP		EDFE CUP	
Start	12	Start	4	Start	2
Replacement	2	Replacement	2	Replacement	0
Sub not used	0	Sub not used	0	Sub not used	0
Replaced	5	Replaced	2	Replaced	1
Try	0	Try	0	Try	0
Conversion	0	Conversion	0	Conversion	0
Penalty goal	0	Penalty goal	0	Penalty goal	0
Drop goal	0	Drop goal	0	Drop goal	0
Total points	0	Total points	0	Total points	0
Red card	0	Red card	0	Red card	0
Yellow card	3	Yellow card	0	Yellow card	0
Won	8	Won	4	Won	1
Drew	0	Drew	0	Drew	1
Lost	6	Lost	2	Lost	0

904 minutes in play	327 minutes in play	116 minutes in play

Alex Brown

PREMIERSHIP		HEINEKEN CUP		EDFE CUP	
Start	16	Start	5	Start	1
Replacement	0	Replacement	0	Replacement	1
Sub not used	1	Sub not used	0	Sub not used	0
Replaced	2	Replaced	1	Replaced	0
Try	0	Try	0	Try	0
Conversion	0	Conversion	0	Conversion	0
Penalty goal	0	Penalty goal	0	Penalty goal	0
Drop goal	0	Drop goal	0	Drop goal	0
Total points	0	Total points	0	Total points	0
Red card	0	Red card	0	Red card	0
Yellow card	0	Yellow card	0	Yellow card	0
Won	11	Won	3	Won	1
Drew	0	Drew	0	Drew	0
Lost	5	Lost	2	Lost	1

1248 minutes in play   332 minutes in play   124 minutes in play

Peter Buxton

PREMIERSHIP		HEINEKEN CUP		EDFE CUP	
Start	14	Start	7	Start	1
Replacement	5	Replacement	0	Replacement	0
Sub not used	0	Sub not used	0	Sub not used	0
Replaced	2	Replaced	2	Replaced	0
Try	0	Try	0	Try	0
Conversion	0	Conversion	0	Conversion	0
Penalty goal	0	Penalty goal	0	Penalty goal	0
Drop goal	0	Drop goal	0	Drop goal	0
Total points	0	Total points	0	Total points	0
Red card	0	Red card	0	Red card	0
Yellow card	0	Yellow card	1	Yellow card	1
Won	13	Won	5	Won	1
Drew	0	Drew	0	Drew	0
Lost	6	Lost	2	Lost	1

1200 min in play   508 minutes in play   70 minutes in play

Christian Califano

PREMIERSHIP		HEINEKEN CUP		EDFE CUP	
Start	2	Start	1	Start	1
Replacement	4	Replacement	3	Replacement	1
Sub not used	4	Sub not used	2	Sub not used	0
Replaced	2	Replaced	2	Replaced	0
Try	0	Try	0	Try	0
Conversion	0	Conversion	0	Conversion	0
Penalty goal	0	Penalty goal	0	Penalty goal	0
Drop goal	0	Drop goal	0	Drop goal	0
Total points	0	Total points	0	Total points	0
Red card	0	Red card	0	Red card	0
Yellow card	0	Yellow card	0	Yellow card	0
Won	5	Won	3	Won	1
Drew	0	Drew	0	Drew	1
Lost	2	Lost	1	Lost	0

179 minutes in play   87 minutes in play   110 minutes in play

Patrice Collazo

PREMIERSHIP		HEINEKEN CUP		EDFE CUP	
Start	4	Start	0	Start	0
Replacement	2	Replacement	1	Replacement	0
Sub not used	1	Sub not used	0	Sub not used	1
Replaced	4	Replaced	0	Replaced	0
Try	0	Try	0	Try	0
Conversion	0	Conversion	0	Conversion	0
Penalty goal	0	Penalty goal	0	Penalty goal	0
Drop goal	0	Drop goal	0	Drop goal	0
Total points	0	Total points	0	Total points	0
Red card	0	Red card	0	Red card	0
Yellow card	0	Yellow card	0	Yellow card	0
Won	4	Won	0	Won	0
Drew	0	Drew	0	Drew	0
Lost	2	Lost	1	Lost	0

301 minutes in play   18 minutes in play

Gareth Cooper

PREMIERSHIP		HEINEKEN CUP		EDFE CUP	
Start	7	Start	1	Start	0
Replacement	7	Replacement	4	Replacement	2
Sub not used	1	Sub not used	0	Sub not used	0
Replaced	5	Replaced	1	Replaced	0
Try	0	Try	0	Try	0
Conversion	0	Conversion	0	Conversion	0
Penalty goal	0	Penalty goal	0	Penalty goal	0
Drop goal	0	Drop goal	0	Drop goal	0
Total points	0	Total points	0	Total points	0
Red card	0	Red card	0	Red card	0
Yellow card	0	Yellow card	0	Yellow card	0
Won	10	Won	3	Won	1
Drew	0	Drew	0	Drew	1
Lost	4	Lost	2	Lost	0
562 minutes in play		113 minutes in play		43 minutes in play	

Gareth Delve

PREMIERSHIP		HEINEKEN CUP		EDFE CUP	
Start	7	Start	4	Start	1
Replacement	4	Replacement	3	Replacement	1
Sub not used	0	Sub not used	0	Sub not used	0
Replaced	5	Replaced	2	Replaced	0
Try	0	Try	1	Try	1
Conversion	0	Conversion	0	Conversion	0
Penalty goal	0	Penalty goal	0	Penalty goal	0
Drop goal	0	Drop goal	0	Drop goal	0
Total points	0	Total points	5	Total points	5
Red card	0	Red card	0	Red card	0
Yellow card	0	Yellow card	0	Yellow card	0
Won	7	Won	5	Won	1
Drew	0	Drew	0	Drew	0
Lost	4	Lost	2	Lost	1

583 minutes in play   395 minutes in play   96 minutes in play

Alasdair Dickinson

PREMIERSHIP		HEINEKEN CUP		EDFE CUP	
Start	1	Start	0	Start	2
Replacement	7	Replacement	1	Replacement	0
Sub not used	1	Sub not used	0	Sub not used	0
Replaced	2	Replaced	0	Replaced	2
Try	0	Try	0	Try	0
Conversion	0	Conversion	0	Conversion	0
Penalty goal	0	Penalty goal	0	Penalty goal	0
Drop goal	0	Drop goal	0	Drop goal	0
Total points	0	Total points	0	Total points	0
Red card	0	Red card	0	Red card	0
Yellow card	0	Yellow card	0	Yellow card	0
Won	7	Won	0	Won	1
Drew	0	Drew	0	Drew	1
Lost	4	Lost	1	Lost	0

197 minutes in play   17 minutes in play   98 minutes in play

James Forrester

Not selected - injured

Jack Forster

PREMIERSHIP		EDFE CUP	
Start	4	Start	1
Replacement	3	Replacement	1
Sub not used	1	Sub not used	0
Replaced	1	Replaced	0
Try	0	Try	0
Conversion	0	Conversion	0
Penalty goal	0	Penalty goal	0
Drop goal	0	Drop goal	0
Total points	0	Total points	0
Red card	0	Red card	0
Yellow card	0	Yellow card	0
Won	5	Won	1
Drew	0	Drew	1
Lost	2	Lost	0

373 minutes in play   112 minutes in play

Mark Foster

PREMIERSHIP		EDFE CUP	
Start	4	Start	3
Replacement	4	Replacement	0
Sub not used	3	Sub not used	0
Replaced	3	Replaced	1
Try	1	Try	0
Conversion	0	Conversion	0
Penalty goal	0	Penalty goal	0
Drop goal	0	Drop goal	0
Total points	5	Total points	0
Red card	0	Red card	0
Yellow card	0	Yellow card	0
Won	5	Won	1
Drew	0	Drew	1
Lost	3	Lost	1

394 minutes in play   215 minutes in play

Andy Hazell

PREMIERSHIP		HEINEKEN CUP		EDFE CUP	
Start	11	Start	1	Start	1
Replacement	0	Replacement	0	Replacement	0
Sub not used	0	Sub not used	0	Sub not used	0
Replaced	1	Replaced	0	Replaced	1
Try	0	Try	0	Try	0
Conversion	0	Conversion	0	Conversion	0
Penalty goal	0	Penalty goal	0	Penalty goal	0
Drop goal	0	Drop goal	0	Drop goal	0
Total points	0	Total points	0	Total points	0
Red card	0	Red card	0	Red card	0
Yellow card	2	Yellow card	0	Yellow card	0
Won	8	Won	0	Won	1
Drew	0	Drew	0	Drew	0
Lost	3	Lost	1	Lost	0

813 minutes in play   80 minutes in play   78 minutes in play

Ali James

PREMIERSHIP			EDFE CUP	
Start	0		Start	1
Replacement	1		Replacement	0
Sub not used	1		Sub not used	0
Replaced	0		Replaced	1
Try	0		Try	0
Conversion	0		Conversion	0
Penalty goal	0		Penalty goal	0
Drop goal	0		Drop goal	0
Total points	0		Total points	0
Red card	0		Red card	0
Yellow card	0		Yellow card	0
Won	0		Won	1
Drew	0		Drew	0
Lost	1		Lost	0

40 minutes in play   79 minutes in play

Will James

PREMIERSHIP		HEINEKEN CUP		EDFE CUP	
Start	9	Start	0	Start	2
Replacement	8	Replacement	2	Replacement	1
Sub not used	2	Sub not used	2	Sub not used	0
Replaced	4	Replaced	0	Replaced	0
Try	0	Try	0	Try	0
Conversion	0	Conversion	0	Conversion	0
Penalty goal	0	Penalty goal	0	Penalty goal	0
Drop goal	0	Drop goal	0	Drop goal	0
Total points	0	Total points	0	Total points	0
Red card	0	Red card	0	Red card	0
Yellow card	2	Yellow card	0	Yellow card	0
Won	11	Won	1	Won	1
Drew	0	Drew	0	Drew	1
Lost	6	Lost	1	Lost	1

734 minutes in play   47 minutes in play   200 minutes in play

Ryan Lamb

PREMIERSHIP		HEINEKEN CUP		EDFE	
Start	16	Start	6	Start	1
Replacement	2	Replacement	1	Replacement	0
Sub not used	1	Sub not used	0	Sub not used	0
Replaced	5	Replaced	2	Replaced	1
Try	4	Try	14	Try	0
Conversion	25	Conversion	13	Conversion	3
Penalty goal	32	Penalty goal	10	Penalty goal	0
Drop goal	1	Drop goal	0	Drop goal	0
Total points	169	Total points	76	Total points	6
Red card	0	Red card	0	Red card	0
Yellow card	2	Yellow card	0	Yellow card	0
Won	13	Won	5	Won	0
Drew	0	Drew	0	Drew	0
Lost	5	Lost	2	Lost	1

1236 min in play   481 minutes in play   70 minutes in play

Rory Lawson

PREMIERSHIP		HEINEKEN CUP		EDFE CUP	
Start	11	Start	6	Start	2
Replacement	4	Replacement	1	Replacement	0
Sub not used	1	Sub not used	0	Sub not used	0
Replaced	7	Replaced	4	Replaced	1
Try	2	Try	1	Try	1
Conversion	0	Conversion	0	Conversion	0
Penalty goal	0	Penalty goal	0	Penalty goal	0
Drop goal	0	Drop goal	0	Drop goal	0
Total points	10	Total points	5	Total points	5
Red card	0	Red card	0	Red card	0
Yellow card	0	Yellow card	0	Yellow card	0
Won	8	Won	5	Won	0
Drew	0	Drew	0	Drew	1
Lost	7	Lost	2	Lost	1

897 minutes in play   467 minutes in play   135 minutes in play

Dave Lewis

PREMIERSHIP		Total points	0
Start	0		
Replacement	1	Red card	0
Sub not used	2	Yellow card	0
Replaced	0		
		Won	1
Try	0	Drew	0
Conversion	0	Lost	0
Penalty goal	0		
Drop goal	0	7 minutes in play	

Leon Lloyd

PREMIERSHIP		HEINEKEN CUP		EDFE CUP	
Start	6	Start	1	Start	1
Replacement	1	Replacement	2	Replacement	0
Sub not used	1	Sub not used	0	Sub not used	0
Replaced	2	Replaced	1	Replaced	0
Try	5	Try	0	Try	0
Conversion	0	Conversion	0	Conversion	0
Penalty goal	0	Penalty goal	0	Penalty goal	0
Drop goal	0	Drop goal	0	Drop goal	0
Total points	25	Total points	0	Total points	0
Red card	0	Red card	0	Red card	0
Yellow card	0	Yellow card	0	Yellow card	0
Won	5	Won	2	Won	1
Drew	0	Drew	0	Drew	0
Lost	2	Lost	1	Lost	0

512 minutes in play   83 minutes in play   80 minutes in play

Ludovic Mercier

PREMIERSHIP

Start	0
Replacement	0
Sub not used	1
Replaced	0
Try	0
Conversion	0
Penalty goal	0
Drop goal	0
Total points	0
Red card	0
Yellow card	0
Won	0
Drew	0
Lost	0

Ross McMillan

Not Selected

Olly Morgan

PREMIERSHIP		HEINEKEN CUP		EDFE CUP	
Start	6	Start	2	Start	2
Replacement	2	Replacement	1	Replacement	0
Sub not used	1	Sub not used	1	Sub not used	0
Replaced	2	Replaced	1	Replaced	1
Try	3	Try	0	Try	1
Conversion	0	Conversion	0	Conversion	0
Penalty goal	0	Penalty goal	0	Penalty goal	0
Drop goal	0	Drop goal	0	Drop goal	0
Total points	15	Total points	0	Total points	5
Red card	0	Red card	0	Red card	0
Yellow card	0	Yellow card	0	Yellow card	0
Won	7	Won	2	Won	1
Drew	0	Drew	0	Drew	0
Lost	1	Lost	1	Lost	1

495 minutes in play	134 minutes in play	151 minutes in play

Luke Narraway

PREMIERSHIP		HEINEKEN CUP		EDFE CUP	
Start	16	Start	4	Start	1
Replacement	4	Replacement	3	Replacement	2
Sub not used	0	Sub not used	0	Sub not used	0
Replaced	6	Replaced	2	Replaced	1
Try	1	Try	1	Try	0
Conversion	0	Conversion	0	Conversion	0
Penalty goal	0	Penalty goal	0	Penalty goal	0
Drop goal	0	Drop goal	0	Drop goal	0
Total points	5	Total points	5	Total points	0
Red card	0	Red card	0	Red card	0
Yellow card	0	Yellow card	1	Yellow card	0
Won	13	Won	5	Won	1
Drew	0	Drew	0	Drew	1
Lost	7	Lost	2	Lost	1
1237 minutes in play		309 minutes in play		107 minutes in play	

Carlos Nieto

PREMIERSHIP		HEINEKEN CUP		EDFE CUP	
Start	17	Start	7	Start	1
Replacement	0	Replacement	0	Replacement	0
Sub not used	0	Sub not used	0	Sub not used	0
Replaced	4	Replaced	1	Replaced	0
Try	0	Try	0	Try	0
Conversion	0	Conversion	0	Conversion	0
Penalty goal	0	Penalty goal	0	Penalty goal	0
Drop goal	0	Drop goal	0	Drop goal	0
Total points	0	Total points	0	Total points	0
Red card	0	Red card	0	Red card	0
Yellow card	1	Yellow card	2	Yellow card	0
Won	12	Won	5	Won	0
Drew	0	Drew	0	Drew	0
Lost	5	Lost	2	Lost	1
1290 minutes in play		521 minutes in play		80 minutes in play	

Dan Norton

PREMIERSHIP

Start	0	Total points	0
Replacement	1		
Sub not used	0	Red card	0
Replaced	0	Yellow card	0
		Won	1
Try	0	Drew	0
Conversion	0	Lost	0
Penalty goal	0		
Drop goal	0	2 minutes in play	

Chris Paterson

PREMIERSHIP		HEINEKEN CUP		EDFE CUP	
Start	3	Start	2	Start	1
Replacement	5	Replacement	4	Replacement	2
Sub not used	1	Sub not used	0	Sub not used	0
Replaced	3	Replaced	3	Replaced	1
Try	1	Try	0	Try	0
Conversion	5	Conversion	4	Conversion	1
Penalty goal	4	Penalty goal	1	Penalty goal	0
Drop goal	0	Drop goal	0	Drop goal	1
Total points	27	Total points	11	Total points	5
Red card	0	Red card	0	Red card	0
Yellow card	0	Yellow card	0	Yellow card	0
Won	4	Won	4	Won	1
Drew	0	Drew	0	Drew	1
Lost	4	Lost	2	Lost	1

305 minutes in play   175 minutes in play   62 minutes in play

Jeremy Paul

PREMIERSHIP		HEINEKEN CUP		EDFE CUP	
Start	1	Start	0	Start	2
Replacement	5	Replacement	1	Replacement	0
Sub not used	2	Sub not used	0	Sub not used	0
Replaced	2	Replaced	1	Replaced	2
Try	0	Try	0	Try	0
Conversion	0	Conversion	0	Conversion	0
Penalty goal	0	Penalty goal	0	Penalty goal	0
Drop goal	0	Drop goal	0	Drop goal	0
Total points	0	Total points	0	Total points	0
Red card	0	Red card	0	Red card	0
Yellow card	0	Yellow card	0	Yellow card	0
Won	3	Won	0	Won	1
Drew	0	Drew	0	Drew	1
Lost	4	Lost	1	Lost	0

142 minutes in play   7 minutes in play   110 minutes in play

Jonathan Pendlebury

PREMIERSHIP		EDFE CUP	
Start	1	Start	0
Replacement	2	Replacement	0
Sub not used	4	Sub not used	1
Replaced	1	Replaced	0
Try	0	Try	0
Conversion	0	Conversion	0
Penalty goal	0	Penalty goal	0
Drop goal	0	Drop goal	0
Total points	0	Total points	0
Red card	0	Red card	0
Yellow card	0	Yellow card	0
Won	2	Won	0
Drew	0	Drew	0
Lost	2	Lost	0

77 minutes in play

Mike Prendergast

PREMIERSHIP		HEINEKEN CUP		EDFE CUP	
Start	5	Start	0	Start	1
Replacement	3	Replacement	1	Replacement	0
Sub not used	4	Sub not used	1	Sub not used	1
Replaced	3	Replaced	0	Replaced	1
Try	0	Try	0	Try	0
Conversion	0	Conversion	0	Conversion	0
Penalty goal	0	Penalty goal	0	Penalty goal	0
Drop goal	0	Drop goal	0	Drop goal	0
Total points	0	Total points	0	Total points	0
Red card	0	Red card	0	Red card	0
Yellow card	0	Yellow card	0	Yellow card	0
Won	6	Won	1	Won	1
Drew	0	Drew	0	Drew	0
Lost	2	Lost	0	Lost	0

374 minutes in play   1 minute in play   62 minutes in play

Karl Pryce

PREMIERSHIP		EDFE CUP	
Start	0	Start	1
Replacement	0	Replacement	0
Sub not used	2	Sub not used	1
Replaced	0	Replaced	1
Try	0	Try	0
Conversion	0	Conversion	0
Penalty goal	0	Penalty goal	0
Drop goal	0	Drop goal	0
Total points	0	Total points	0
Red card	0	Red card	0
Yellow card	0	Yellow card	0
Won	0	Won	0
Drew	0	Drew	1
Lost	0	Lost	0

30 minutes in play

Akapusi Qera

PREMIERSHIP		HEINEKEN CUP		EDFE CUP	
Start	12	Start	6	Start	2
Replacement	2	Replacement	0	Replacement	0
Sub not used	0	Sub not used	0	Sub not used	0
Replaced	7	Replaced	2	Replaced	2
Try	5	Try	3	Try	0
Conversion	0	Conversion	0	Conversion	0
Penalty goal	0	Penalty goal	0	Penalty goal	0
Drop goal	0	Drop goal	0	Drop goal	0
Total points	25	Total points	15	Total points	0
Red card	0	Red card	0	Red card	0
Yellow card	0	Yellow card	1	Yellow card	0
Won	8	Won	5	Won	0
Drew	0	Drew	0	Drew	1
Lost	6	Lost	1	Lost	1
890 minutes in play		431 minutes in play		95 minutes in play	

Charlie Sharples

PREMIERSHIP			
PREMIERSHIP		Total points	0
Start	1		
Replacement	1	Red card	0
Sub not used	1	Yellow card	0
Replaced	1		
		Won	1
Try	0	Drew	0
Conversion	0	Lost	1
Penalty goal	0		
Drop goal	0	80 minutes in play	

James Simpson-Daniel

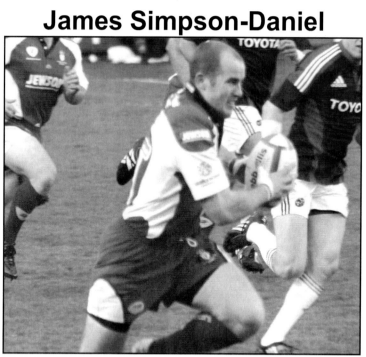

PREMIERSHIP		HEINEKEN CUP		EDFE CUP	
Start	8	Start	7	Start	2
Replacement	0	Replacement	0	Replacement	1
Sub not used	0	Sub not used	0	Sub not used	0
Replaced	1	Replaced	0	Replaced	0
Try	10	Try	3	Try	2
Conversion	0	Conversion	0	Conversion	0
Penalty goal	0	Penalty goal	0	Penalty goal	0
Drop goal	0	Drop goal	0	Drop goal	0
Total points	50	Total points	15	Total points	10
Red card	0	Red card	0	Red card	0
Yellow card	0	Yellow card	0	Yellow card	0
Won	13	Won	5	Won	1
Drew	0	Drew	0	Drew	1
Lost	5	Lost	2	Lost	1

1436 minutes in play	560 minutes in play	162 minutes in play

Alasdair Strokosch

PREMIERSHIP		HEINEKEN CUP		EDFE CUP	
Start	14	Start	4	Start	3
Replacement	6	Replacement	2	Replacement	0
Sub not used	0	Sub not used	0	Sub not used	0
Replaced	5	Replaced	3	Replaced	1
Try	0	Try	1	Try	0
Conversion	0	Conversion	0	Conversion	0
Penalty goal	0	Penalty goal	0	Penalty goal	0
Drop goal	0	Drop goal	0	Drop goal	0
Total points	0	Total points	5	Total points	0
Red card	0	Red card	0	Red card	0
Yellow card	0	Yellow card	0	Yellow card	0
Won	13	Won	5	Won	1
Drew	0	Drew	0	Drew	1
Lost	7	Lost	1	Lost	1

1190 minutes in play   346 minutes in play   222 minutes in play

Mike Tindall

PREMIERSHIP		HEINEKEN CUP	
Start	13	Start	6
Replacement	0	Replacement	1
Sub not used	0	Sub not used	0
Replaced	4	Replaced	3
Try	3	Try	1
Conversion	0	Conversion	0
Penalty goal	0	Penalty goal	0
Drop goal	0	Drop goal	0
Total points	15	Total points	5
Red card	0	Red card	0
Yellow card	0	Yellow card	0
Won	11	Won	5
Drew	0	Drew	0
Lost	2	Lost	2

889 minutes in play   486 minutes in play

Andy Titterrell

PREMIERSHIP		HEINEKEN CUP		EDFE CUP	
Start	12	Start	2	Start	0
Replacement	7	Replacement	5	Replacement	3
Sub not used	1	Sub not used	0	Sub not used	0
Replaced	12	Replaced	2	Replaced	0
Try	1	Try	1	Try	0
Conversion	0	Conversion	0	Conversion	0
Penalty goal	0	Penalty goal	0	Penalty goal	0
Drop goal	0	Drop goal	0	Drop goal	0
Total points	5	Total points	5	Total points	0
Red card	0	Red card	0	Red card	0
Yellow card	0	Yellow card	0	Yellow card	0
Won	13	Won	5	Won	1
Drew	0	Drew	0	Drew	1
Lost	6	Lost	2	Lost	1

854 minutes in play   226 minutes in play   78 minutes in play

Henry Trinder

PREMIERSHIP

Start	0	Total points	0
Replacement	1	Red card	0
Sub not used	0	Yellow card	0
Replaced	0		
		Won	0
Try	0	Drew	0
Conversion	0	Lost	1
Penalty goal	0		
Drop goal	0	17 minutes in play	

Dan Tuohy

PREMIERSHIP

Start	2
Replacement	0
Sub not used	2
Replaced	1
Try	0
Conversion	0
Penalty goal	0
Drop goal	0
Total points	0
Red card	0
Yellow card	1
Won	1
Drew	0
Lost	1

145 minutes in play

Lesley Vainikolo

PREMIERSHIP		HEINEKEN CUP		EDFE CUP	
Start	12	Start	5	Start	0
Replacement	0	Replacement	0	Replacement	1
Sub not used	0	Sub not used	0	Sub not used	0
Replaced	2	Replaced	0	Replaced	0
Try	9	Try	2	Try	0
Conversion	0	Conversion	0	Conversion	0
Penalty goal	0	Penalty goal	0	Penalty goal	0
Drop goal	0	Drop goal	0	Drop goal	0
Total points	45	Total points	10	Total points	0
Red card	0	Red card	0	Red card	0
Yellow card	0	Yellow card	0	Yellow card	0
Won	8	Won	4	Won	0
Drew	0	Drew	0	Drew	0
Lost	4	Lost	1	Lost	1

904 minutes in play	400 minutes in play	25 minutes in play

Willie Walker

PREMIERSHIP		HEINEKEN CUP		EDFE CUP	
Start	12	Start	0	Start	1
Replacement	6	Replacement	3	Replacement	1
Sub not used	3	Sub not used	1	Sub not used	0
Replaced	1	Replaced	0	Replaced	0
Try	1	Try	1	Try	0
Conversion	12	Conversion	0	Conversion	1
Penalty goal	16	Penalty goal	0	Penalty goal	0
Drop goal	1	Drop goal	0	Drop goal	3
Total points	80	Total points	5	Total points	11
Red card	0	Red card	0	Red card	0
Yellow card	0	Yellow card	0	Yellow card	0
Won	11	Won	2	Won	1
Drew	0	Drew	0	Drew	1
Lost	7	Lost	1	Lost	0

1091 min in play   69 minutes in play   118 minutes in play

Nick Wood

PREMIERSHIP		HEINEKEN CUP		EDFE CUP	
Start	18	Start	6	Start	1
Replacement	1	Replacement	0	Replacement	0
Sub not used	0	Sub not used	0	Sub not used	0
Replaced	8	Replaced	2	Replaced	0
Try	1	Try	0	Try	0
Conversion	0	Conversion	0	Conversion	0
Penalty goal	0	Penalty goal	0	Penalty goal	0
Drop goal	0	Drop goal	0	Drop goal	0
Total points	5	Total points	0	Total points	0
Red card	0	Red card	0	Red card	0
Yellow card	0	Yellow card	0	Yellow card	0
Won	12	Won	5	Won	0
Drew	0	Drew	0	Drew	0
Lost	7	Lost	1	Lost	1

1334 minutes in play   463 minutes in play   80 minutes in play

PRE-SEASON

MIDDLESEX SEVEN-A-SIDE
Twickenham
16 August 2007

GLOUCESTER SQUAD

Luke Narraway (**captain and coach**), Ross McMillan, Jack Adams, James Bailey, Karl Pryce, Mark Foster, Dan Norton, Pete Swatkins, Dave Lewis, Ludovic Mercier, Dan Copsey, Jordi Pasqualin

Pool 1
London Wasps
Gloucester Rugby
Worcester Warriors

10.45am Round 1
Gloucester Rugby 19 – 10 London Wasps

Gloucester Rugby	London Wasps
Try Norton (2); Adams (2)	**Try** Cipriani
Con Mercier (2)	

1.35pm Round 2
Gloucester Rugby 7 – 24 Worcester Warriors

Gloucester Rugby	Worcester
Try: Swatkins Wood	**Try:** Pennell (2) Delport
Con: Swatkins	**Con:** Drahm (2)

76

3.05pm Quarter Final
Gloucester Rugby 33 – 14 Leeds Carnegie

Gloucester Rugby Carnegie	**Leeds**
Try: Foster (3) Norton Narraway	**Try:** Myall (2)
Con: Foster (3) Bailey	**Con:** Hinton Myall

4.45pm Semi Final
Gloucester Rugby 5 – 26 Newcastle Falcons

Gloucester Rugby	**Newcastle Falcons**
Try: Pasqualin	**Try:** Phillips (2) Fielden Dixon
	Con: Fielden (2)

Cardiff Blues 40 – 10 Gloucester Rugby

Arms Park
Saturday 25 August 2007

CARDIFF BLUES
15. N Macleod 14. B Blair 13. T Selley 12. M Stcherbina 11. R Williams 10. D Flanagan 9. J Spice 8. X Rush **(captain)** 7. R Sowden-Taylor 6. M Molitika 5. P Tito 4. D Jones 3. G Powell 2. G Williams 1. J Yapp

Replacements
16. R Gill 17. R Johnson 18. B Davies 19. M Lewis 20. R Rees 21. N Robinson 22. D Hewitt 23. S Roberts 24. R Sidoli 25. B White 26. T Riley

GLOUCESTER RUGBY
15. I Balshaw 14. M Foster 13. L Lloyd 12. A Allen 11. L Vainikolo 10. R Lamb 9. M Prendergast 1. P Collazo 2. O Azam **(captain)** 3. C Califano 4. J Pendlebury 5. A Brown 6. A Strokosch 7. A Hazell 8. L Narraway

Replacements
16. A Titterrell 17. A Dickinson 18. N Wood 19. D Tuohy 20. D Williams 21. D Lewis 22. W Walker 23. A James 24. O Morgan

There was a three-hour delay in kick off time due to roadworks and bank holiday traffic on the M4 motorway so nobody treated this result very seriously.

The team coach was forced to take a detour through Monmouth, delaying the kick off from 2.30pm to 5.15pm and there is a difference between a team being forced to sit on a coach, sweating and stewing for a period of time approaching five hours and a team calmly awaiting a home match, sitting in the cool of the changing room, waiting for their opposition to arrive.

There might have been a time, twenty-odd years ago, when Cardiff could conceivably have been thirty points better than Gloucester – but not these days.

Ollie Azam was Gloucester's captain, his first time in the role and nine new recruits to the Gloucester banner were blooded. Lesley Vainikolo was called on to play on the left wing, opposite ex-All Black winger Ben Blair.

Leon Lloyd, fresh from Leicester, partnered Anthony Allen in the centre, and scrum-half Mike Prendergast, from Bourgoin, partnered Ryan Lamb in

the halves. Scotland international, Alexander Strokosch, was the only new

face in the forwards, playing blindside flanker for us, while Andy Hazell and Luke Narraway took the openside and number eight berths respectively.

With club captain Marco Bortolami and Will James away on World Cup duty for Italy and Wales respectively, Jonathan Pendlebury joined Alex Brown in the second row.

Dan Tuohy, former Ireland under-21 lock, made his appearance in the senior squad for the first time.

Cardiff opened the scoring with a try by hooker, Gareth Williams, from a catch-and-drive following a penalty kick for a Gloucester infringement. Blair converted and the score was Cardiff Blues 7 – 0 Gloucester Rugby.

Gloucester got on the scoreboard when Ryan Lamb intercepted a pass in the Gloucester 22 and sprinted 80 metres downfield to touch down under the Cardiff posts.

The conversion for him was a mere formality and the scores were level at Cardiff Blues 7 – 7 Gloucester Rugby.

A few minutes later Lamb got on the scoreboard once again when he kicked Gloucester into the lead with Gloucester's first penalty of the season to move the score on to Cardiff Blues 7 – 10 Gloucester Rugby.

Half time score Cardiff Blues 7 – 10 Gloucester Rugby

Cardiff came out for the second half with guns blazing but seemed incapable of capitalising on their field position to actually score.

Five minutes into the half saw a chance for them to draw level with a penalty but Blair sent his kick wide and at least three try-scoring opportunities for Cardiff went begging before they elected to scrummage five metres out, following a penalty decision.

Replacement Daffyd Hewitt chose an unstoppable line and Robinson added the conversion to move the score on to Cardiff Blues 12 – 10 Gloucester Rugby.

Cardiff's next try came from an individual effort by Macleod. He kicked through from his own half, safely gathering the ball to touch down for Robinson to make the easy conversion. With the score at Cardiff 19 – 10 Gloucester, it looked as though Gloucester were running out of steam. A point borne out by the fact that we conceded five of Cardiff's six tries in the last half-hour of the match.

The next score came when Rush broke through the Gloucester defence and fed Rhys Williams who somehow beat three defenders to score. The conversion sailed over and the score was Cardiff Blues 26 – 10 Gloucester Rugby.

Cardiff's fifth try came soon after when a tapped penalty put Lewis into space, allowing him to score under the posts. Once more the conversion was a formality and the score moved on to Cardiff Blues 33 – 10 Gloucester Rugby.

A couple of minutes from the end White scored Cardiff's last try, again it

was converted and the game finished at Cardiff Blues 40 – 10 Gloucester Rugby.

Hazell took a bang on the arm late in the game but it was not believed to be serious and he was expected to make the second and final warm up match against Ulster at Ravenhill on 8 September.

Ulster 19 – 23 Gloucester Rugby

Ravenhill
Kick off 6.30pm Saturday 8 September 2007

Willie Walker opened the scoring with a penalty to put Gloucester in the lead at Ulster 0 – 3 Gloucester Rugby but the home team drew level when Ulster's Paul Steinmetz slotted a penalty to put the match level at Ulster 3 – 3 Gloucester Rugby.

Before the first quarter of the match had ended Gloucester winger James Bailey touched down for the first try of the evening which Walker duly converted to put Gloucester in the lead by seven points at Ulster 3 – 10 Gloucester Rugby.

But on the twenty six-minute mark Paul Steinmetz notched up his second penalty to pull three points closer at Ulster 6 – 10 Gloucester Rugby.

On the half-hour mark the home team pulled clear when O'Connor touched down for a try after a breakaway against the run of play.

This time Steinmetz was unable to make his kick tell and the score stayed at Ulster 11 – 10 Gloucester Rugby.

Determined to take the lead back before the break, Gloucester's Willie Walker added a drop goal to put his side back in the lead at Ulster 11 – 13 Gloucester Rugby.

Half time score Ulster 11 – 13 Gloucester

Gloucester were given a chance to increase their lead with a penalty but Walker was unable to capitalise.

Then, six minutes into the half, Ulster fullback Bryn Cunningham crossed our line to touch down and put his team back in the lead at Ulster 16 – 13 Gloucester Rugby. Once more the home team failed to convert and that is how the score stayed.

Gloucester levelled the game at Ulster 16 – 16 Gloucester Rugby when replacement Ryan Lamb knocked over a penalty but Ulster were proving a hard nut to crack when a few minutes later Steinmetz scored another penalty to put his team in the lead at Ulster 19 – 16 Gloucester Rugby.

That was to prove the last score of the match for Steinmetz - who was stretchered off the field suffering a concussion after a Vainikolo tackle – and for Ulster, despite the fact that they staged a last quarter rally after a match strewn with questionable decision-making and unforced errors.

But it was to no avail. With fifteen minutes to go Pete Buxton touched down to put Gloucester back in the lead at Ulster 19 – 21 Gloucester Rugby and Lamby added the conversion to close the match at Ulster 19 – 23 Gloucester Rugby,

Leeds Carnegie 24 - 49 Gloucester Rugby

Kick off 3.00pm Sunday 16 September 2007
Attendance 10,674 : David Rose referee

LEEDS CARNEGIE

15. J Goodridge 14. T Rock 13. J Hepworth 12. R Welding 11. T Biggs 10. A di Bernardo 9. J Bedford 1. M Cusack 2. R Rawlinson 3. C Noon 4. S Hooper 5. K Myall 6. J Dunbar 7. H Fourie 8. R Oakley

Replacements

16. A Hopcroft 17. J Parkes 18. P Bouza 19. M Lock 20. J Brooks 21. J Holtby 22. L Hinton

GLOUCESTER RUGBY

15. I Balshaw 14. J Simpson-Daniel 13. L Lloyd 12. A Allen 11. L Vainikolo
10. R Lamb 9. M Prendergast 1. P Collazo 2. O Azam 3. C Nieto 4. J Pendlebury 5. A Brown 6. P Buxton 7. A Hazell 8. L Narraway

Replacements

16. A Titterrell 17. C Califano 18. D Tuohy 19. A Strokosch 20. D Lewis 21. L Mercier 22. O Morgan

Left wing Lesley Vainikolo put down his marker in our first competitive match of the season. He created space, made his tackles and finished with awe-inspiring power. A fact borne out by his personal tally of five tries from Gloucester's bag of eight.

It was Leeds' first game back in the Premiership, having been replaced in Division One by Northampton and in front of their biggest crowd ever. They were full of hope and ambition... and we hammered 'em!

The home side showed signs of nerves which led to a number of penalties being awarded our way. With the wind behind us we kicked for the corners and opened the scoring with only four minutes on the clock when Ryan Lamb took the play to the right and passed out to Leon Lloyd who shipped a long pass out to Sinbad who came into the line to make the extra man and finished with his usual cold-blooded efficiency, crossing for the first score of the day.

The windy conditions put paid to our conversion attempt and the score stayed at Leeds Carnegie 0 – 5 Gloucester.

Two minutes later the home side responded with a try of their own through Dunbar. It was a gift as he beat Bucko, Prendergast and Balshaw down the blindside of a ruck and di Bernardo added the conversion to give his side the lead at Leeds Carnegie 7 – 5 Gloucester Rugby.

On fourteen minutes di Bernardo added a penalty when Andy Hazell was adjudged to be offside and four minutes later the Argentinian repeated the feat to put his side even further in the lead at Leeds 13 Carnegie – 5 Gloucester Rugby.

Then, with twenty seven minutes on the clock, we scored our second try of the day when Lamb saw some space and threw a speculative pass to Balshaw who did not waste the opportunity to score against his old club. Again, the wind put paid to our conversion attempt and the score stayed at Leeds Carnegie 13 – 10 Gloucester but five minutes later Lamb added a penalty to put the match all square at Leeds Carnegie 13 – 13 Gloucester Rugby.

We were strong in our set pieces, denying the home side possession from that area, although we made mistakes and gifted them possession on a number of occasions, but we were strong enough, through the likes of Andy Hazell, and later Alasdair Strokosch, to turn over a lot of their possession and we were able and confident to move the ball about and pull defenders out of position.

However, two minutes later di Bernardo put his side back in front at Leeds Carnegie 16 – 13 Gloucester with another penalty but on the thirty six minute mark Vainikolo crossed for his first try when he scored from a re-start.

Azam threw a long pass infield where Lloyd and Balshaw combined to take it up. It is true that the touchline can often be your best defender and Leeds sought to use this strategy but it was a major error as they failed to factor Vainikolo into the equation. He galloped up, ran straight over the top of Leeds' winger Tom Rock – reducing him to rubble in the process – and his momentum carried him over the line with four defenders desperately trying to pull him down..

Premiership try lines are the best defended in the world but how do you defend against an irresistible force? When Vainikolo scored that try there was a sharp intake of breath from the Premiership clubs which could be heard throughout the length and breadth of England rugby.

At Leeds Carnegie 16 – 18 Gloucester Rugby , the Premiership was left in no doubt: Big Les had arrived in rugby union.

Once more we failed to add the conversion and on the forty minute mark Brooks, who had replaced di Bernardo, slotted a penalty to put his team back in the lead again at Leeds Carnegie 19 – 18 Gloucester Rugby.

Half time score Leeds Carnegie 19 – 18 Gloucester Rugby

Four minutes into the second half we regained the lead through an Anthony Allen try. It ensued from a kickable penalty which we elected to kick into touch instead, *via* Ryan Lamb. When it was released Lamby sent Allen through a gap to touch down under the posts.

Ryan Lamb effortlessly added the conversion to increase our lead to Leeds Carnegie 19 – 25 Gloucester Rugby.

Five minutes later ex-Gloucester fullback Jon Goodridge helped set up a try for Rock after he linked up with Welding. They could not add the conversion and we stayed in the lead by a single point at Leeds Carnegie 24 – 25 Gloucester Rugby.

We made a number of substitutions: on fifty one minutes Titterrell replaced Azam and seven minutes later Strokosch came on for Pendlebury then two minutes later Big Les struck again right on the hour mark when we turned over possession and Allen took it up before passing to Lamb who shipped it on to Narraway.

A long pass outside found Vainikolo who touched down in the corner, moving the score on to Leeds Carnegie 19 – 30 Gloucester Rugby. Lamb's conversion attempt rebounded off the post but six minutes later Big Les went over for his hat trick – again from turnover ball – when Hazell took it up with Sinbad and Balshaw in support. Again Vainikolo's pace and momentum did the trick and the score moved to Leeds Carnegie 24 – 35 Gloucester Rugby. Lamb added the conversion and it was Leeds Carnegie 24 – 37 Gloucester Rugby.

Big Les' fourth try came when Lamb put in a perfectly-weighted cross kick which he fielded effortlessly and touched down to put the score at an unassailable Leeds Carnegie 24 – 42 Gloucester Rugby.

It was all over bar the shouting, but Vainikolo still had another try in him. What works once will work again, and two minutes

from full time Lamb put in another cross kick for Big Les to gather. He threw one, two dummies inside and then crossed for his fifth try.
Lamb added the conversion and the match ended at a shell-shocked Leeds Carnegie 24 – 49 Gloucester Rugby. One match gone and we were top of the league.

LEEDS CARNEGIE
Try: Dunbar, Rock
Conversion: di Bernardo
Penalty goal: Brooks;
di Bernardo (3)

GLOUCESTER
Try: Allen, Balshaw, Simpson-Daniel, Vainikolo 5
Conversion: Lamb 3
Penalty goal: Lamb

OTHER RESULTS
Bath Rugby 29 - 15 Worcester Warriors
Harlequins 35 - 27 London Irish
London Wasps 19 - 29 Saracens
Bristol Rugby 13 - 26 Leicester Tigers
Newcastle Falcons 33 - 12 Sale Sharks

CLUB	P	W	D	L	F	A	TF	TA	TB	LB	P
Gloucester Rugby	1	1	0	1	49	24	8	2	1	0	5
Newcastle Falcons	1	1	0	1	33	12	4	2	1	0	5
Bath Rugby	1	1	0	1	29	15	4	2	1	0	5
Harlequins	1	1	0	1	35	27	4	3	1	0	5
Leicester Tigers	1	1	0	1	13	2	2	1	0	0	4
Saracens	1	1	0	1	29	19	3	1	0	0	4
London Irish	1	0	0	0	27	35	3	4	0	0	0
London Wasps	1	0	0	0	19	29	1	3	0	0	0
Bristol Rugby	1	0	0	0	13	26	1	2	0	0	0
Worcester Warriors	1	0	0	0	15	29	2	4	0	0	0
Sale Sharks	1	0	0	0	12	33	2	4	0	0	0
Leeds Carnegie	1	0	0	0	24	49	2	8	0	0	0

Guinness Premiership
Round Two
Vicarage Road
Saracens 31 – 38 Gloucester Rugby
Kick off 3.00pm Sunday 23 September 2007
Attendance 6,976 : M Fox referee

SARACENS
15. D Scarbrough 14. R Penney 13. K Sorrell 12. A Powell 11. F Leonelli 10. G Ross 9. N de Kock 1. N Lloyd 2. M Cairns   3. T Mercey 4. T Ryder 5. H Vyvyan 6. K Chesney 7. R Hill 8. B Skirving

Replacements
16. A Kyriacou 17. K Yates 18. P Gustard 19. D Seymour 20. A Dickens 21. C McMullen 22. E Thrower

GLOUCESTER RUGBY
15. I Balshaw 14. J Simpson-Daniel 13. L Lloyd 12. A Allen 11. L Vainikolo 10. R Lamb 9. M Prendergast 1. N Wood 2. A Titterrell 3. C Nieto 4. P Buxton 5. A Brown 6. A Strokosch 7. A Hazell 8. L Narraway

Replacements
16. O Azam 17. C Califano 18. J Pendlebury 19. A Balding 20. D Lewis 21. W Walker 22. O Morgan

Another four-try exhibition to give us maximum league points for the second week running. Could there be a better way to start a season?

We opened the scoring with a Ryan Lamb penalty four minutes into the game but three minutes later Saracens drew level at Saracens 3 – 3 Gloucester Rugby when Ross retaliated.   Then four minutes later a Saracens try by Powell came from a line out drive. Ross broke through our defence and moved it on to Scarbrough who made the scoring pass to Powell. This put them in the lead at Saracens 8 – 3 Gloucester Rugby then six minutes later they went even further ahead at Saracens 11 – 3 Gloucester Rugby when Powell kicked another penalty.

With twenty three minutes on the clock we notched up our second score of the day - a penalty - courtesy of Ryan Lamb.

Three minutes later Hazey got himself yellow-carded when the referee concluded that his tackle on Ross was late.

Reduced to fourteen men we still managed to add to our score when Lamb knocked over another penalty to move the score along to Saracens 11 – 6 Gloucester Rugby.

Anthony Allen scored a try when Big Les took the ball dangerously close to the Saracens left corner flag and quick ball was worked to the right where Simpson-Daniel sent Allen over to tie the score at Saracens 11 – 11 Gloucester. Lamb added the conversion to put us in the lead by two points at Saracens 11 – 13 Gloucester Rugby.

With forty minutes on the clock Lamb slotted his fifth kick and fourth penalty to put us in the lead by five points at Saracens 11 – 16 Gloucester Rugby.

Then just before half time we added another Lamb penalty to give us an eight point lead at the interval.

Half time score Saracens 11 – 19 Gloucester Rugby

Six minutes into the second half saw Saracens score their first try. It came through Sorrell after Leonelli pierced the Gloucester defence on our twenty two before laying off the ball to centre Kevin Sorrell. The try was converted by Ross, moving the score on to Saracens 21 – 19 Gloucester Rugby.

Six minutes later we struck back with a try through Ryan Lamb. Sustained pressure from Saracens was looking distinctly dangerous inside our twenty two when Lamb intercepted a pass from Ross intended for lock Hugh Vyvyan. Haring up the pitch for eighty-odd metres he beat Scarbrough to the line to score under the posts.

"If you cannot convert your own tries, whose can you convert?", ask the old men and Lamby showed he was more than capable of converting his own tries as he moved the scoreline on to Saracens 21 – 26 Gloucester Rugby.

One minute later Ollie Azam came on for Andy Titterrell and four minutes later Olly Morgan replaced Big Les who went off with a neck injury. After his breathtaking performance the previous week against Leeds Lesley failed to make so much impact on this match, although he did have a hand in Anthony Allen's try.

One minute later Allen took a pass from Prendergast and broke down the left. From the ensuing ruck Narraway picked his chance and picked the ball. Breaking through the Saracens defence he touched down behind the posts. Lamby converted it to put us nicely in charge of the match at Saracens 21 – 33 Gloucester Rugby.

At sixty five minutes Saracens glimpsed a way of winning the match when Thrower scored a try, which was converted by Ross to move them closer at Saracens 28 – 33 Gloucester Rugby but Olly Morgan landed the bonus point for four tries scored when Willie Walker, who had replaced Lamb, combined with Prendergast and Lloyd to release Morgan.

The conversion attempt failed and Saracens got a losing bonus point from the match when Ross kicked another penalty two minutes into injury time.

	SARACENS	GLOUCESTER

SARACENS
Try: Powell, Sorrell, Thrower
Conversion: Ross (2)
Penalty goal: Ross (4)

GLOUCESTER
Try: Allen, Morgan, Lamb, Narraway
Conversion: Lamb (3)
Penalty goal: Lamb (4)

OTHER RESULTS
Leicester Tigers 26 - 16 Bath Rugby
Harlequins 39 - 15 Leeds Carnegie
Worcester Warriors 24 - 24 London Wasps
London Irish 19 - 0 Newcastle Falcons
Sale Sharks 20 - 6 Bristol Rugby

CLUB	P	W	D	L	F	A	TF	TA	TB	LB	P
Gloucester Rugby	2	2	0	0	87	55	12	5	2	0	10
Harlequins	2	2	0	0	74	42	9	5	2	0	10
Leicester Tigers	2	2	0	1	52	29	4	2	0	0	8
Bath Rugby	2	1	0	1	45	41	5	4	1	0	5
Saracens	2	1	0	1	60	57	6	5	0	1	5
Newcastle Falcons	2	1	0	1	33	31	4	4	1	0	5
London Irish	2	1	0	1	46	35	5	4	0	0	4
Sale Sharks	2	1	1	1	32	39	3	4	0	0	4
London Wasps	2	0	1	1	43	53	3	6	0	0	2
Worcester Warriors	2	0	0	2	39	53	5	6	0	0	2
Bristol Rugby	2	0	0	2	19	46	1	3	0	0	0
Leeds Carnegie	2	0	0	2	39	88	4	13	0	0	0

Gloucester Rugby 29 – 7 Worcester Warriors

Kick off 6.00pm Saturday 29 September 2007
Attendance 15,781 : D Rose referee

GLOUCESTER RUGBY
15. O Morgan 14. J Simpson-Daniel 13. M Tindall 12. A Allen 11. J Bailey 10. R Lamb 9. M Prendergast 1. N Wood 2. O Azam 3. C Nieto 4. P Buxton 5. A Brown 6. A Strokosch 7. A Hazell 8. L Narraway

Replacements
16. A Titterrell 17. C Califano 18. J Pendlebury 19. A Balding 20. D Lewis 21. W Walker 22. K Pryce

WORCESTER WARRIORS
15. S Drahm 14. T Delport 13. D Rasmussen 12. D Feau'nati 11. M Garvey 10. J Brown 9. R Powell 1. D Morris 2. C Fortey 3. T Taumoepeau 4. P Murphy 5. C Gillies 6. D Hickey 7. P Sanderson 8. K Horstmann

Replacements
16. T Windo 17. B Gotting 18. W Bowley 19. G Quinnell 20. M Powell 21. M Tucker 22. C Pennell

Before a capacity crowd we celebrated the opening of the new C&G Grandstand with a scintillating performance which reinforced our position at the top of the league with a three-try victory over our near neighbours from Sixways. Mike Tindall returned from an enforced five-month absence after suffering a broken leg and it was great to see such Shed favourites from the past as Thinus Delport, Marcel Garvey, Chris Fortey and evergreen Tony "Reg" Windo on such fine form.

Worcester's new hand on the tiller, Mike Ruddock, seemed to have instilled a new dimension to their game with added venom at the set pieces and sharp handling in the backs.

At half time we went in six points to nil up, courtesy of two Ryan Lamb penalties on thirty one minutes and forty minutes, although we did also manage to miss two eminently kickable opportunities.

The first half was a knock-'em-down-drag-'em-out slugfest between the two

committed forward packs who contested the set pieces and the contact area as if their lives depended on it.

Television commentators would say it was not a thing of beauty unless you happened to be a dyed in the wool Shedhead in which case the dour struggle for supremacy was a forty minute epic.

As luck would have it, the crowd was full of the latter and with shining eyes and soaring spirits we licked our lips in anticipation of the second half.

Half time score Gloucester Rugby 6 – 0 Worcester Warriors

Three minutes into the half Lamby put us further ahead with a well-struck penalty to put us nine points ahead but for those whose preference is for running rugby, the game sprang to life with seven minutes of the second half ticked off the clock.

A long pass out to the left found its way into the hands of James Simpson-Daniel who took off along the touchline. He ran around Rasmussen as if he was not there, outwitted Thinus Delport – not an easy accomplishment – and accelerated away to touch down as he pleased.

At Gloucester Rugby 14 – 0 Worcester Warriors, Ryan Lamb stepped up for the conversion and added the two points to put us sixteen points to nil ahead.

With fifty seven minutes on the clock Gavin Quinnell came on as a substitute. It was an imaginative decision as he scored Worcester's only try one minute later when his side won a lineout close to the Gloucester line.

He chose a direct line over Alex Brown and touched down with Andy Hazell in very close attendance but unable to remove Quinnell's grip from the ball. Drahm added the conversion and the score moved on to Gloucester Rugby 16 – 7 Worcester Warriors.

A minute later ex-Gloucester legend Tony Windo replaced Morris but Worcester's hopes of a renaissance were short-lived because two minutes later Browner won a lineout and from the ensuing drive Oli Azam was admirably placed to touch it down for our second try of the day. Lamby missed the conversion attempt and the score stayed at Gloucester Rugby 21 – 7 Worcester Warriors.

With ten minutes to go Titterrell replaced Azam and three minutes later Lamb kept on the pressure when Sanderson was yellow-carded in the tackle area and the ensuing play resulted in an elegantly taken drop goal which increased our lead to Gloucester Rugby 24 – 7 Worcester Warriors. At the same time Lewis came on for Prendergast and Balding replaced Narraway.

Then one minute from time Lamb chipped the ball behind the defence. Sinbad and Tindall were quickly up and Marcel made a hash of his defence which resulted in Tindall touching down for the day's final score:

Gloucester Rugby 29 – 7 Worcester Warriors. Four more league points in the bag.

GLOUCESTER RUGBY	WORCESTER WARRIORS
Try: Azam, Tindall, S-Daniel	**Try:** Quinnell
Conversion: Lamb	**Conversion:** Drahm
Penalty Goal: Lamb (3)	
Drop goal: Lamb	

OTHER RESULTS
Bath Rugby 21 - 19 Sale Sharks
Newcastle Falcons 19 - 12 Harlequins
Bristol Rugby 14 - 11 London Irish
Leeds Carnegie 7 - 31 Saracens
London Wasps 17 - 20 Leicester Tigers

CLUB	P	W	D	L	F	A	TF	TA	TB	LB	P
Gloucester Rugby	3	3	0	0	116	62	15	6	2	0	14
Leicester Tigers	3	3	0	0	72	46	5	3	0	0	12
Harlequins	3	2	0	1	86	61	9	8	2	1	11
Saracens	3	2	0	1	91	64	10	6	1	1	10
Newcastle Falcons	3	2	0	1	52	43	7	4	1	0	9
Bath Rugby	3	2	0	1	66	60	7	5	1	0	9
London Irish	3	1	0	2	57	49	6	5	0	1	5
Sale Sharks	3	1	0	2	51	60	4	6	0	1	5
Bristol Rugby	3	1	0	2	33	57	2	4	0	0	4
London Wasps	3	0	1	2	60	73	4	7	0	1	3
Worcester Warriors	3	0	1	2	46	82	6	9	0	0	2
Leeds Carnegie	3	0	0	3	46	119	5	17	0	0	0

Leicester Tigers 17 – 30 Gloucester Rugby

Kick off 6.00pm Saturday 6 October 2007
Attendance 17,101 : R Maybank referee

LEICESTER TIGERS

15. G Murphy 14. J Murphy 13. O Smith 12. M Cornwell 11. T Varndell 10. A Goode 9. F Murphy 1. A Moreno 2. B Kayser 3. J White 4. L Deacon 5. M Wentzel 6. B Deacon 7. L Abraham 8. J Crane

Replacements

16. M Davies 17. M Castrogiovanni 18. R Blaze 19. T Croft 20. B Youngs 21. P Burke 22. A Erinle

GLOUCESTER RUGBY

15. O Morgan 14. L Lloyd 13. M Tindall 12. A Allen 11. J Bailey 10. W Walker 9. M Prendergast 1. P Collazo 2. O Azam 3. C Nieto 4. P Buxton 5. A Brown 6. A Strokosch 7. A Hazell 8. L Narraway

Replacements

16. A Titterrell 17. C Califano 18. N Wood 19. W James 20. G Cooper 21. R Lamb 22. M Foster

To go to Welford Road and come away with a convincing victory; and to be unlucky not to have scored more; and to have forced the home side to elect for a lineout because they were so comprehensively outgunned in the pack; and to put clear blue water between ourselves and the league runners-up; how good an afternoon's sport was that?

It started only three minutes into the match when Leicester were controlling the centre of the pitch. Goode broke to his left and threw out a long pass. Unfortunately for him we were fielding Leon Lloyd who can read his old team like a book. He picked the pass out of mid air and hared downfield to score a try to a stunned and silent stadium. Which brought a smile to every Gloucester supporter's face but none of them as wide as

93

the smile lighting up Lloyd's face as he trotted back over the halfway line.

After the match he wryly commented: "That was the best pass I have had from Goodey in about twelve years".

Willie Walker added the conversion and at Leicester Tigers 0 – 7 Gloucester Rugby, we were starting to build a score.Goode partially redeemed himself on the thirteen minute mark with a penalty kick which put them four points closer at Leicester Tigers 3 – 7 Gloucester Rugby but his place kicking still let him down twice in the first half.

The same could not be said about Willie Walker. Four minutes later he kicked a penalty to put us seven points clear at Leicester Tigers 3 – 10 Gloucester Rugby. The kick was awarded for Leicester going over the top at a lineout drive.

With twenty three minutes on the clock came the seminal act of the match. Walker sent a kick through which caused the home side no end of problems. Resulting in them conceding a five metre scrum.

Moreno was guilty of boring into Nieto and the referee had no hesitation in awarding a penalty try. Suffice to say there have been more popular refereeing decisions at Welford Road...

Walker added the afters and the scoresheet read Leicester Tigers 3 – 17 Gloucester Rugby.

Eight minutes later Walker added yet another penalty to his formidable collection and at Leicester Tigers 3 – 20 Gloucester Rugby the sides went in for the break.

Half time score Leicester Tigers 3 – 20 Gloucester Rugby

Ten minutes into the second half Gloucester failed to grasp an opportunity to kill the game off. Anthony Allen flicked a pass back through his legs and Narraway took it on the burst. He passed to Bailey who passed it on to Buxton who looked as if he touched it down. The video referee said otherwise, though, ruling that Leicester had kept it up and we gave away a free kick from the ensuing scrummage.

Walker did slot another penalty to put us even further ahead at Leicester Tigers 3 – 23 Gloucester Rugby but we could not manage to score a try.

On another occasion a long kick deep into Leicester territory had Varndell scurrying back to cover but he conceded a lineout from which replacement scrum half Gareth Cooper crossed the line and touched down but the referee said the last pass had gone forward.

With fifty six minutes gone Nick Wood replaced Patrice Collazo and four minutes later Croft replaced Anthony Allen.

With ten minutes to go Leicester broke through and scored a try care of Tom Croft. Paul Burke who had replaced Goode at half time added the conversion.

The score stood at Leicester Tigers 10 – 23 Gloucester Rugby and the match was set for a thrilling finale. Seven minutes before the end of ordinary time Leicester conceded a lineout deep in their twenty two and the Gloucester forwards ominously rolled it slowly but relentlessly forward.

When the time came Walker took his chance and avoiding the cover, he crashed over for Gloucester's third try which he cheerfully converted, accounting for a personal tally of twenty points for the day and the scoreline read Leicester Tigers 10 – 30 Gloucester Rugby.

Three minutes later Califano replaced Nieto and then right at the death Leicester showed how dangerous they can be, even without their international players who were away on a Six Nations weekend. Our defence was sound all afternoon but still Matt Cornwell was able to elude Narraway and score for the home side.

Burke converted and the referee blew the final whistle at Leicester Tigers 17 – 30 Gloucester Rugby.

The last word on the game should go to Leon Lloyd who said, "When I played here for Leicester about a hundred and fifty-odd times, I think we only lost about five or six times. So I know how hard it is to win here."

LEICESTER TIGERS
Try: Cornwell, Croft
Conversion: Burke (2)
Penalty Goal: Goode

GLOUCESTER RUGBY
Try: Lloyd, Walker
Conversion: Walker (3)
Penalty Goal: Walker (3)

OTHER RESULTS
Sale Sharks 16 - 0 London Wasps
London Irish 20 - 22 Bath Rugby
Newcastle Falcons 21 - 19 Leeds Carnegie
Harlequins 24 - 18 Bristol Rugby
Worcester Warriors 16 - 21 Saracens

CLUB	P	W	D	L	F	A	TF	TA	TB	LB	P
Gloucester Rugby	4	4	0	0	146	79	18	8	2	0	18
Harlequins	4	3	0	1	110	79	12	10	2	1	15
Saracens	4	3	0	1	112	80	12	7	1	1	14
Newcastle Falcons	4	3	0	1	73	62	9	6	1	0	13
Bath Rugby	4	3	0	1	88	80	10	6	1	0	13
Leicester Tigers	4	3	0	1	89	76	7	6	0	0	12
Sale Sharks	4	2	0	2	67	60	5	6	0	1	9
London Irish	4	1	0	3	77	71	7	8	0	2	6
Bristol Rugby	4	1	0	3	51	81	4	7	0	1	5
London Wasps	4	0	1	3	60	89	4	8	0	1	3
Worcester Warriors	4	0	1	3	62	103	7	11	0	1	3
Leeds Carnegie	4	0	0	4	65	140	7	19	0	1	1

Gloucester Rugby 31 – 12 Sale Sharks

Kick off 3.00pm Saturday 13 October 2007
Attendance 14,075 : A Rowden referee

GLOUCESTER RUGBY

15. O Morgan 14. L Lloyd 13. M Tindall 12. A Allen 11. J Bailey 10. R Lamb 9. R Lawson 1. N Wood 2. A Titterrell   3. C Nieto 4. W James 5. A Brown 6. P Buxton 7. A Strokosch   8. L Narraway

Replacements

16. O Azam 17. C Califano 18. M Bortolami 19. A Qera 20. M Prendergast 21. W Walker 22. I Balshaw

SALE SHARKS

15. B Foden 14. J Laharrague 13. R Keil 12. El Seveali'i 11. O Ripol Fortuny 10. C Hodgson 9. S Martens 1. L Faure 2. M Jones 3. B Bourrust 4. D Schofield 5. S Cox 6. C Jones 7. M Lund 8. G Fessia

Replacements

16. S Lawson 17. B Evans 18. D Tait 19. J White 20. R Wigglesworth 21. R Jones 22. C Bell

Another display of set piece superiority from Gloucester paved the way for our fifth win on the trot.

Sale opened the scoring with a try after only five minutes. We were forced to defend a lineout drive which developed into a midfield maul from which their tighthead, Bourrust, burst over with no real challenge. Gloucester Rugby 0 – 5 Sale Sharks. Hodgson failed with his conversion attempt.

On twelve minutes we were awarded a penalty when Sale were adjudged to have handled in the ruck and Ryan Lamb opened our account at Gloucester Rugby 3 – 5 Sale Sharks

A short period of sustained pressure resulted in Sale being penalised for playing the ball off their feet in a ruck and Lamby duly put us in front at Gloucester Rugby 6 – 5 Sale Sharks on the twenty three minute mark.

Eight minutes later he slotted over another after Sale infringed following a Gloucester cross field kick, putting the score at Gloucester Rugby 9 – 5 Sale Sharks and he added a fourth six minutes later to increase our lead to seven points at Gloucester Rugby 12 – 5 Sale Sharks.

It would have been a respectable score with which to go into the break but

it was not to be. With forty minutes on the clock though, Sale cancelled out

our lead with a try when Foden and Laharrague broke down the left wing.

The French winger singled out our tighthead Carlos Nieto in the defensive line and beat him easily before shipping the ball on to Ripol Fortuny who evaded tackles from Lamby and Leon Lloyd before crossing our line for their only try of the day. Hodgson's conversion, which tied the half time score at Gloucester Rugby 12 – 12 Sale Sharks, was to prove to be their last score, not only of the half but of the match as well.

As the half drew to a close Christian Califano temporarily replaced Nick Wood.

Half time score Gloucester Rugby 12 – 12 Sale Sharks

One minute into the second half saw Sale's Sean Cox yellow carded and Gloucester took full advantage of the extra man. Nick Wood came back onto the pitch to replace Califano and it was a good job he did, too. Because two minutes later we drove our lineout infield and as it appeared to come to a standstill, Wood made a deft pass out to Lloyd who scooted home to move the score on to Gloucester Rugby 17 – 12 Sale Sharks and Lamb added the conversion to move us two points further ahead at Gloucester Rugby 19 – 12 Sale Sharks.

A small matter of two minutes later we scored another try. This time it was initiated by Allen who made a break down the centre of the field before passing to Tindall who gave the scoring pass to Lloyd who crossed the visitors' line for his third try in two matches for Gloucester at which Gloucester supporters exchanged approving glances. Lamb was unable to add the conversion but at Gloucester Rugby 24 – 12 Sale Sharks we were starting to look quite comfortable.

Our forwards continually knocked them back in the contact area and individually the work ethic of our big forwards could not be faulted - another point which was not lost on the knowing Gloucester support.

With an hour and three minutes on the clock Azam came on to replace Titterrell and add even more grunt to the Gloucester effort and Balshaw replaced Lloyd. Three minutes later we crossed for our third try when Lamb put a kick downfield which sat up beautifully for the chasing Balshaw, he caught the ball and fed Olly Morgan who was coming on the burst. Morgan screamed over the line behind the posts to put the score at Gloucester Rugby 29 – 12 Sale Sharks, making Lamb's conversion attempt a mere formality and the score moved on to Gloucester Rugby 31 – 12 Sale Sharks.

It looked as if we had scored our fourth try when Allen made a break and fed Balshaw but the referee ruled the pass was forward.

With sixty six minutes gone Sale's Bell replaced ex-Gloucester player Rudi Keil and one minute later Califano came on for Nick Wood and a minute after that Willie Walker replaced Ollie Morgan. To be followed one minute later by Bortolami replacing Will James who had worked ceaselessly all afternoon.

Seven minutes from time Qera replaced Tindall and we played the game

out at Gloucester Rugby 31 – 12 Sale Sharks.

Dean Ryan could have made kinder comments in the post-match press conference."I thought we were too individual, particularly in the first-half, and as an overall performance I thought it was our worst of the season," he said.

He was right of course, but our earlier performances would have proved extremely difficult for any team to constantly live up to.

GLOUCESTER RUGBY	SALE SHARKS
Try: Lloyd (2) Morgan	**Try:** R Fortuny, Bourrust
Conversion: Lamb (2)	**Conversion:** Hodgson
Penalty Goal: Lamb (4)	

OTHER RESULTS
Leeds Carnegie 26 - 21 Worcester Warriors
Bath Rugby 25 - 10 Harlequins
Bristol Rugby 23 - 16 Newcastle Falcons
London Wasps 28 - 14 London Irish
Saracens 26 - 19 Leicester Tigers

CLUB	P	W	D	L	F	A	TF	TA	TB	LB	P
Gloucester Rugby	5	5	0	0	177	91	21	10	2	0	22
Saracens	5	4	0	1	138	99	15	9	1	1	18
Bath Rugby	5	4	0	1	113	90	13	7	1	0	17
Harlequins	5	3	0	2	120	104	13	13	2	1	15
Newcastle Falcons	5	3	0	2	80	85	10	8	1	1	14
Leicester Tigers	5	3	0	2	108	102	9	9	0	1	13
Sale Sharks	5	2	0	3	79	91	7	9	0	1	9
Bristol Rugby	5	2	0	3	74	97	6	8	0	1	9
London Wasps	5	1	1	3	88	103	7	9	0	1	7
London Irish	5	1	0	4	91	99	8	11	0	2	6
Leeds Carnegie	5	1	0	4	91	161	10	21	0	1	5
Worcester Warriors	5	0	1	4	83	129	9	14	0	2	4

London Irish 15 – 10 Gloucester Rugby

Kick off 4.00pm Sunday 21 October 2007
Attendance 7,582 : S Davey referee

LONDON IRISH

15. P Hewat 14. T Ojo 13. D Armitage 12. S Mapusua 11. T de Vedia 10. S Geraghty 9. P Hodgson 1. D Murphy   2. D Paice 3. T Lea'aetoa 4. N Kennedy 5. B Casey 6. K Roche 7. D Danaher 8. P Murphy

Replacements

16. T Warren 17. D Coetzee 18. G Johnson 19. R Thorpe 20. S Armitage 21. W Fury 22. J Staunton

GLOUCESTER RUGBY

15. I Balshaw 14. C Paterson 13. M Tindall 12. A Allen 11. J Bailey 10. R Lamb 9. M Prendergast 1. P Collazo   2. A Titterrell 3. C Califano 4. M Bortolami 5. A Brown 6. P Buxton 7. A Qera 8. L Narraway

Replacements

16. O Azam 17. A Dickinson 18. W James 19. A Strokosch 20. R Lawson 21. W Walker 22. K Pryce

The thing about winning sequences is they have to come to an end and that is what happened to our glorious winning start to the season on a Sunday afternoon in Reading.

Our downfall began when we pulled down Kennedy at a lineout after three minutes play. Hewat slotted the difficult kick and we were behind at London Irish 3 – 0 Gloucester Rugby.

The Irish game plan was simple but effective: pile in at the breakdown and slow things down; keep our back three turning with the kick through. These tactics worked so effectively that we were never able to establish any rhythm and it was to cost us dearly in terms of frustration for individual players and our unbeaten record as a team.

Ryan Lamb was yellow carded after twenty one minutes for attempted robbery at the breakdown and although it had no direct impact on the match this setback did serve to slow down our game even further.

We had one chance to draw level when we were awarded a penalty. Chris Paterson on his Gloucester debut stepped up to take the kick but was unable to convert the chance into points on the scoreboard and so the game staggered along to half time.

Half time score London Irish 3 – 0 Gloucester Rugby

We needed some sort of platform early in the second half but it was not to be. Four minutes into the half Geraghty angled a low, dangerous kick through our defence and de Vedia pounced on it to score a try to put his side further ahead at London Irish 8 – 0 Gloucester Rugby.

Hewat added the conversion and at London Irish 10 – 0 Gloucester Rugby, things were pretty bleak, considering the shape the game had taken.

But it was not all doom and gloom. ten minutes into the half Bucko followed up a Prendergast box kick and made it safe, for the first time that afternoon we had quick ball and we took full advantage. Prendergast took control again and got the ball to Bailey who passed to Balshaw.

Balshaw chipped through and chased and caught his own kick, colliding with Hodgson, who was sent sprawling, his way to the line was clear. We were back in the game at London Irish 10 – 5 Gloucester Rugby.

This time Paterson made no mistake with his kick and at London Irish 10 – 7 Gloucester Rugby things should have been brightening up for us but we were still unable to impose ourselves on the game.

With fifty four minutes gone we substituted Lawson for Prendergast and eleven minutes later Will James came on for Marco Bortolami and four minutes later Azam replaced Titterrell and Dickinson came on for Collazo all to no avail.

Eight minutes from time Irish scored their second try, again from a Geraghty kick through. It was designed for Ojo who somehow contrived to miss the ball completely as he went over the top of it but de Vedia made no mistake and touched down for his second try of the day to take the score on to London Irish 15 – 7 Gloucester Rugby.

Two minutes later Paterson slotted his second penalty to put us closer at London Irish 15 – 10 Gloucester Rugby and Strokosch replaced Qera.

Dean Ryan's post-match comments: "There wasn't a fast ball or a ruck that didn't have people all over it and that meant the scoreline was always going to be tight.
"There was no quick phase ball in the game and it meant we couldn't move cohesively."

LONDON IRISH	GLOUCESTER RUGBY
Try: de Vedia (2)	**Try:** Balshaw,
Conversion: Hewat	**Conversion:** Paterson
Penalty Goal: Hewat	**Penalty Goal:** Paterson

OTHER RESULTS
Sale Sharks 34 - 30 Saracens
Harlequins 26 - 25 London Wasps
Leicester Tigers 28 - 20 Worcester Warriors
Newcastle Falcons 20 - 33 Bath Rugby
Bristol Rugby 39 - 13 Leeds Carnegie

CLUB	P	W	D	L	F	A	TF	TA	TB	LB	P
Gloucester Rugby	6	5	0	1	187	106	22	12	2	1	23
Bath Rugby	6	5	0	1	146	110	18	9	2	0	22
Saracens	6	4	0	2	168	133	18	13	1	2	19
Harlequins	6	4	0	2	146	129	15	16	2	1	19
Leicester Tigers	6	4	0	2	139	122	12	11	0	1	17
Bristol Rugby	6	3	0	3	113	110	11	9	1	1	14
Sale Sharks	6	3	0	3	113	121	11	12	1	1	14
Newcastle Falcons	6	3	0	3	109	118	12	13	1	1	14
London Irish	6	2	0	4	106	109	10	12	0	0	10
London Wasps	6	1	1	4	113	129	10	11	0	0	8
Leeds Carnegie	6	1	0	5	104	200	11	26	0	0	5
Worcester Warriors	6	0	1	5	103	157	11	17	0	0	4

Gloucester Rugby 18 – 18 Newcastle Falcons

Kick off 3.00pm Saturday 27 October 2007
Attendance 10,358 : B Robertson (England) referee

GLOUCESTER RUGBY

15. I Balshaw 14. K Pryce 13. J Simpson-Daniel 12. A Allen
11. M Foster 10. C Paterson 9. R Lawson 1. A Dickinson 2. J
Paul 3. C Califano 4. W James 5. M Bortolami 6. A Strokosch
7. A Qera 8. A Balding

Replacements
16. A Titterrell 17. J Forster 18. J Pendlebury 19. L Narraway
20. G Cooper 21. W Walker 22. J Bailey

NEWCASTLE FALCONS

15. T May 14. O Phillips 13. T Visser 12. S Jones 11. J Rudd
10. T Flood 9. H Charlton 1. J McDonnell 2. M Thompson 3. D
Wilson 4. A Perry 5. M Sorenson 6. G Parling 7. B Wilson 8. R
Winter

Replacements
16. A Long 17. M Ward 18. J Oakes 19. E Williamson 20. J
Grindal 21. A Tait 22. A Dehaty

It took Newcastle two whole minutes to engineer their first
score. Scrumhalf Hall Charlton fed Flood who shipped out a
long pass to Phillips who ran it in with consummate ease.
Gloucester Rugby 0 – 5 Newcastle Falcons. Flood added the
conversion and we were seven points down at Gloucester
Rugby 0 – 7 Newcastle before we had even broken sweat.
A couple of minutes later we had an excellent opportunity to
open our account when Paterson put in a towering kick which
Flood spilled. The Gloucester support, led by Qera burst onto
the ball and moved it down the leftfield but we contrived to
knock it forward. From the ensuing scrum their winger Rudd
knocked it on and Allen pounced on the loose ball. He was
pulled down a matter of inches from the Newcastle line.

There were eighteen minutes on the clock before Gloucester finally managed to get on the scoreboard when Paterson moved the score on to Gloucester Rugby 3 – 7 Newcastle Falcons, following the award of a penalty for Newcastle being off their feet in a ruck.

Despite that incident, it was clear that their control in the contact area was

superior to our own. We also struggled in the lineout, an area where we had experienced all sorts of difficulties the previous week against London Irish.

Winger Karl Pryce never looked comfortable. He was slow on the turn and reluctant to get involved at all. It was impossible to tell if he was injured but it came as no great surprise when he was replaced by James Bailey on the half-hour mark and a few minutes later Jeremy Paul was replaced by Andy Titterrell when our lineout confusion refused to improve.

Two minutes from the break Newcastle struck again. Flood put in a very dangerous chip and chase, Bailey gathered but was hunted down by Rudd and was penalised when he declined to release the ball. Newcastle kicked for the corner and the inevitable catch-and-drive resulted in hooker Matt Thompson being driven over, making the score Gloucester Rugby 3 – 12 Newcastle Falcons. And that is how they went in for the break.

Half time score Gloucester Rugby 3 – 12 Newcastle Falcons

We started the half by making a number of substitutions. Two minutes in Willie Walker replaced Paterson and six minutes later Forster replaced Dickinson, followed by the substitution of Qera with Narraway and Lawson with Cooper on the fifty five minute mark.

With an hour on the clock Walker bagged our second penalty of the day, cutting the visitors' lead to six points at Gloucester Rugby 6 – 12 Newcastle Falcons but our small incursion into their lead was wiped out one minute later when Flood knocked over a penalty to put his team further ahead at Gloucester Rugby 6 – 15 Newcastle Falcons and a couple of minutes later he repeated the trick to put them even further ahead at Gloucester Rugby 6 – 18 Newcastle Falcons.

With only twelve minutes left on the clock we finally made the breakthrough we had been searching for. Bortolami tapped back off the top of a lineout, Cooper executed a beautiful long, flat pass to Walker who made space for Sinbad to race to the line for a touchdown. Walker converted and we were back in the game at Gloucester Rugby 13 – 18 Newcastle Falcons.

Suddenly the game was energised in our favour as forwards and backs began operating with purpose and spirit. From their first half inability to make an impact the Gloucester side began to function as individuals, although they still did not meld as a unit.

There were dangerous attacks from the likes of Allen, Balshaw and Qera as we constantly crossed the gainline and there was one heart stopping moment when Newcastle could still have won the match. Their fullback May kicked through, putting himself in acres of space and he chased up quickly but he made a dog's breakfast of retrieving the ball and the danger passed.

Finally our big forwards, notably Balding and James, set an attack in motion which Balshaw, Simpson-Daniel and Bailey assisted and when the ball came back quickly, via Cooper and Walker, Newcastle had run out of tacklers and Simpson-Daniel was left with the duty of touching down to put the scores level at Gloucester Rugby 18 – 18 Newcastle Falcons.

It was down to Walker to win the match with his conversion attempt but it failed and honours were even with both teams taking away two points and Gloucester's interest in the EDF Energy Cup still very much alive and kicking.

However, ours had been a performance lacking cohesion. Despite the fact that we had controlled great swathes of the game and created a number of scoring chances we had failed to perform as a team; finally depending on individual skills to pull us through, as in the previous week's match against London Irish.

Our set piece problems at the lineout had now spread to the scrum as well and this drawn match raised as many questions as it answered.

GLOUCESTER RUGBY	NEWCASTLE FALCONS
Try: S-Daniel (2)	**Try:** Phillips, Thompson
Conversion: Walker	**Conversion:** Flood
Penalty Goal: Paterson, Walker	**Penalty Goal:** Flood (2)

OTHER POOL A RESULT
Gwent Dragons 3 – 3 London Wasps

Position	Club	Played	Points
1	Gloucester Rugby	1	2
2	Gwent Dragons	1	2
3	London Wasps	1	2
4	Newcastle Falcons	1	2

London Wasps 29 – 26 Gloucester Rugby

Kick off 3.00pm Sunday 4 November 2007
Attendance 7,802 : W Barnes (England) referee

LONDON WASPS

15. D Cipriani 14. P Sackey 13. F Waters 12. R Hoadley 11. T Voyce 10. R Flutey 9. E Reddan 1. T Payne 2. J Ward   3. N Adams 4. Skivington   5. R Birkett 6. D Leo 7. T Rees   8. L Dallaglio

Replacements
16. R Ibanez 17. M Holford 18. J Hart 19. J Haskell 20. S Amor 21. D Walder 22. M van Gisbergen

GLOUCESTER RUGBY

15. O Morgan 14. I Balshaw 13. J Simpson-Daniel12. A Allen 11. M Foster 10. R Lamb 9. R Lawson 1. N Wood   2. O Azam 3. C Nieto 4. P Buxton   5. A Brown 6. A Strokosch   7. A Qera 8. L Narraway

Replacements
16. A Titterrell 17. P Collazo 18. W James 19. G Delve 20. M Prendergast 21. C Paterson 22. L Vainikolo

How do you manage to snatch defeat from the jaws of victory when you are eighteen points clear going into the last quarter? The clues were visible in our two previous matches if only we had been prepared to see them but this game started so well for us how could we possibly know that the taste of victory against last season's Heineken Cup winners would turn to ashes in our mouths?

We opened the scoring after four minutes with a Lawson try when he darted over from the base of a ruck. Lamb converted and it was London Wasps 0 – 7 Gloucester Rugby.

In many respects this score typified the half for us as we played forty minutes of intelligent heads-up rugby. We had a couple of try-scoring chances but in the event we had to wait until the thirty fifth minute before our next score.

Our halves, Lamb and Lawson, got the ball close to our visitors' line and a couple of muscle-straining forward drives resulted in a try being awarded. Oli Azam was the last to emerge and as he had possession of the ball the try was awarded to him.

Once more Lamb added the conversion and the score stood at a convincing London Wasps 0 – 14 Gloucester Rugby.

On the forty minute mark Cipriani landed a penalty for Wasps and we went in for the break at London Wasps 3 – 14 Gloucester Rugby.

Half time score London Wasps 3 – 14 Gloucester Rugby

Seven minutes into the second half Ollie Morgan scored our third try of the afternoon when Lamb sent Narraway through a gap on our opponents' twenty two metre line. Cipriani scrambled back to make a try-saving tackle but Lawson and Lamb got the ball to Sinbad who gave the scoring pass to Morgan who touched down to make the score London Wasps 3 – 19 Gloucester Rugby. Lamb sent the conversion over the bar straight and true and we were beginning to congratulate ourselves on a job well done at London Wasps 3 – 21 Gloucester Rugby. We thought the match was over – but how often does sport flatter only to deceive in the cruellest fashion imaginable?

Twelve minutes into the half Titterrell replaced Azam and two minutes later Wasps struck with a try through Tom Voyce. Following a break by Waters, Voyce broke Simpson-Daniel's tackle and moved the score on to London Wasps 8 – 21 Gloucester Rugby.

The home team failed in their conversion attempt and one minute later Vainikolo was brought on to replace Mark Foster.

The Wasps score obviously inspired the home support but when we scored a fourth try it looked to all intents and purposes as if the match was won.

At a minute past the hour mark Narraway won the ball at the tail of a lineout and it went out to our backs. Lamb sent a long, long pass outside - a Wasps supporter would say the pass was forward – but Ollie Morgan came into the line, seized the ball and the opportunity, and sent Balshaw off and running towards the opposition line.

Touching down, Balshaw moved the scoreline on to Wasps 8 – 26 Gloucester Rugby. Lamb was unable to score with his conversion attempt but with nineteen minutes left on the clock and an eighteen points advantage, what could go wrong? All we needed to do was stay cool, calm and collected and control the game. Could we accomplish that small thing?

Not really. Wasps responded to Ibanez's call to rally round the flag and they slowly but inexorably increased the pressure and Gloucester started to crumble. Haskell was driven over our line after a series of strength-sapping drives in the sixty fourth minute and Cipriani added the conversion as Gareth Delve replaced Luke Narraway in our back row. At London Wasps 15 – 26 Gloucester Rugby the character of the match subtly changed in favour of our opponents.

Five minutes later Pete Buxton got himself yellow carded when he tapped the ball away from ex-Gloucester player Simon Amor and with only fourteen Gloucester men on the pitch Lamb was replaced by Paterson as our game plan was changed to draw the sting of Wasps attacks with long-range defensive kicks to pin Wasps down in their own half.

But the best laid plans of mice and men *etc* and with nine minutes left Wasps' pressure was converted into points when Haskell crossed our line again. At London Wasps 20 – 26 Gloucester Rugby, the writing was on the wall and when Cipriani scored with his conversion attempt, moving the score on to London Wasps 22 – 26 Gloucester Rugby, there was a feeling that a fourth Wasps try was an inevitability.

Sure enough with three minutes left on the clock Ibanez peeled off the back of a lineout, Haskell helped him out and found Hart with his pass.

The ball was moved to Voyce and as he crossed our line and touched down their fourth try he plunged a dagger into the hearts of the travelling Gloucester support.

At London Wasps 27 – 26 Gloucester Rugby the conversion was immaterial but Cipriani added insult to injury when his kick sailed over the crossbar to put the score at London Wasps 29 – 26 Gloucester Rugby.

For over an hour we competed with them physically, which is not the easiest of tasks by any stretch of the imagination. We scrummaged like demons and our decision-making was extraordinary yet we still could not manage to squeeze out a victory, an issue which is not new to us but for all that, one which we sometimes find it difficult to overcome.

We were left wondering what effect this defeat would have on our European efforts.

LONDON WASPS
Try: Haskell (2), Voyce (2)
Conversion: Cipriani (3)
Penalty Goal: Cipriani

GLOUCESTER RUGBY
Try: Azam, Balshaw, Lawson, Morgan
Conversion: Lumb (3)

OTHER POOL A RESULT
Newcastle Falcons 29 - 24 Gwent Dragons

Position	Club	Played	Points
1	Newcastle Falcons	2	7
2	London Wasps	2	7
3	Gloucester Rugby	2	4
4	Gwent Dragons	2	4

Heineken Cup Pool Two
Ravenhill
Ulster 14 – 32 Gloucester Rugby
8.00pm kick off Friday 9 November 2007
Attendance 13,000 : N Owens (Wales) referee

ULSTER

15. B Cunningham 14. T Bowe 13. A Trimble 12. R Dewey 11. M McCrea 10. P Wallace 9. I Boss 1. J Fitzpatrick 2. R Best 3. B Young 4. J Harrison 5. C del Fava 6. M McCullough 7. N Best 8. R Wilson

Replacements

16. N Brady 17. D Fitzpatrick 18. R Caldwell 19. K Dawson 20. K Campbell 21. D Humphreys 22. M Bartholomeusz

GLOUCESTER RUGBY

15. I Balshaw 14. J Simpson-Daniel 13. M Tindall 12. A Allen 11. L Vainikolo 10. R Lamb 9. R Lawson 1. N Wood 2. O Azam 3. C Nieto 4. P Buxton 5. A Brown 6. A Strokosch 7. A Qera 8. L Narraway

Replacements

16. A Titterrell 17. C Califano 18. M Bortolami 19. G Delve 20. M Prendergast 21. C Paterson 22. O Morgan

It was redemption time at Ravenhill as the Gloucester Boys sought to put the mistakes of their previous match, when they threw away certain victory against Wasps, behind them.

Twenty nine points to nil inside the first half hour of play. That is how good we were; racking up our score at a rate of one point per minute. We capitalised on every mistake they made – and that was plenty – and got a bonus point to boot. In other words we wreaked havoc at Ravenhill.

Our first try came after eight minutes when Balshaw worked his way through a defensive gap and shipped on to Narraway who made ground up the middle of the pitch. Tindall and Lamb took it on before Qera made progress down the middle into the Ulster twenty two. The ball came back and Lamby sent a kick through for Vainikolo to touch down. We missed the conversion attempt but it was still Ulster 0 – 5 Gloucester Rugby.

Two minutes later we won a scrum on our five metre line and what followed was the play of the match, if not the season.

Lamb decided to run it, then passed to Tindall, who kept up the momentum. Balshaw put some pace on it and off-loaded to Simpson-Daniel who had cruised up on his outside. Sinbad sent the ball back inside to Balshaw who passed it on to Tindall who was left with the task of racing standoff half Paddy Wallace to the line. Once more we missed the conversion but the score now stood at Ulster 0 – 10 Gloucester Rugby and Ulster were reeling back on their heels as Gloucester reinforced their statement of intent in the strongest manner possible.

With a quarter of an hour gone Gloucester were fired up when Narraway broke from the back of a scrum. Qera took the pass and took it over the gainline before releasing the Gloucester backs.

Lamb chose his line and touched down for try number three. The conversion attempt went astray again but the score stood at a more than creditable Ulster 0 – 15 Gloucester Rugby.

But we were just getting into our stride. With twenty three minutes gone, Wallace was put under pressure from an Ulster scrum and we turned over possession. Lamb went forward with it – what else would you do with turnover ball? But the speedy Ulster backs were closing him down as he shipped it on to Simpson-Daniel who had more than enough gas in the tank to beat the winger Tommy Bowe and touch down in the corner.

At Ulster 0 – 20 Gloucester Rugby, the bonus point was safe and Lamb made no mistake with the conversion, moving the score on to Ulster 0 – 22 Gloucester Rugby.

We were still hungry for more, though. Our fifth try came courtesy of Iain Balshaw. Again it came from turnover ball and when the ball came to Simpson-Daniel he fed Balsh who completed the formality. Lamb added the conversion and at Ulster 0 – 29 Gloucester Rugby, we looked home and hosed.

The home side should have hung out the white flag by this time but there came a point when we failed to clear our lines effectively and their tighthead prop carried it back up to us.

When the ball was recycled, Boss, Wallace and Trimble contrived to break away and very nearly put Trimble over, but that required one more phase of play to accomplish.

The Irishmen threw in as many bodies as they could find and blindside McCullough was driven over for the try. At Ulster 5 – 29 Gloucester Rugby. Wallace slotted the conversion, moving the score on to Ulster 7 – 29 Gloucester Rugby.

But there was still time for them to score a second try before half time.

Following their first period of sustained pressure, Wallace broke past Tindall and touched down, right on the forty minute mark. At Ulster 12 – 29 Gloucester Rugby he added the conversion to his try and the referee blew for half time at Ulster 14 – 29 Gloucester Rugby.

Half time score Ulster 14 – 29 Gloucester Rugby

If only the second half had lived up to the promise of the first, but it did not
and Gloucester were forced to defend for sustained periods. Although we
were denied possession for long periods of time we defended faultlessly with the forwards driving back wave after wave of attackers.

In the sixty eighth minute Lamb kicked a further three points when we were awarded a penalty and that is how the match closed, with the score at Ulster 14 – 32 Gloucester Rugby.

It was a match which showed the Gloucester team off to their best advantage. The first half was an exhibition of intensity and concentration contrasted with a second half of determination and dogged tackling.

It was a great performance and a great evening for Gloucester Rugby.

ULSTER	GLOUCESTER RUGBY
Try: McCullough, Wallace	**Try:** Balshaw, Lamb, S-Daniel, Tindall, Vainikolo
Conversion: Wallace (2)	**Conversion:** Lamb (2)
	Penalty Goal: Lamb

OTHER POOL 2 RESULT
Ospreys 22 - 15 Bourgoin

Position	Club	Played	Points
1	Gloucester Rugby	1	5
2	Ospreys	1	4
3	Bourgoin	1	1
4	Ulster	1	0

Kingsholm
Gloucester Rugby 26 – 18 Ospreys
Kick off 8.00pm Friday 16 November 2007
Attendance 16,500 : G Clancy (Ireland) referee

GLOUCESTER RUGBY
15. I Balshaw 14. J Simpson-Daniel 13. M Tindall 12. A Allen 11. L Vainikolo 10. R Lamb 9. R Lawson 1. N Wood 2. O Azam 3. C Nieto 4. P Buxton 5. M Bortolami 6. A Strokosch 7. A Qera 8. L Narraway

Replacements
16. A Titterrell 17. C Califano 18. W James 19. G Delve 20. M Prendergast 21. C Paterson 22. O Morgan

OSPREYS
15. L Byrne 14. N Walker 13. S Parker 12. G Henson 11. J Vaughton 10. J Hook 9. M Phillips 1. D Jones 2. H Bennett 3. A Jones 4. I Gough 5. I Evans 6. J Thomas 7. M Holah 8. F Tiatia

Replacements
16. R Hibbard 17. P James 18. A-W Jones 19. H T-Pole 20. J Marshall 21. S Connor 22. M Taylor

This match was as ferocious and determined as you could wish for an Anglo-Welsh European Cup encounter to be.

The Ospreys came off the starting blocks the better of the two teams and sought to subject us to early pressure, but Gloucester refused to be intimidated and with eight minutes on the clock opted to attack from a deep position. It was the wrong option.

Tindall put an awkward pass out to Balshaw who was unable to take possession. Walker – the Ospreys winger - pounced on the ball which came back to Hook who gave the scoring pass to Parker.

Hook added the two points for the conversion and it was Gloucester Rugby 0 – 7 Ospreys.

With twelve minutes gone Ryan Lamb kicked a penalty which reduced the visitors' lead to four points at Gloucester Rugby 3 – 7 Ospreys and ten minutes later he kicked another penalty for three more points, putting the score at Gloucester Rugby 6 – 7 Ospreys.

During this period Gloucester were forced to defend for long periods against the unrelenting Ospreys pressure.

The Welsh fury finally took its toll when Holah, who had continually asked
questions of our defence, took it up the middle, Phillips kept up the momentum and it was left to Parker to score his second try by outwitting Nieto and Allen and avoiding Tindall's cover tackle by a whisker. Hook missed his conversion attempt but at Gloucester Rugby 6 – 12 Ospreys another score in the Welshmen's favour would have put Gloucester in a world of hurt.

As it happened Lamby added another penalty to his collection minutes into first half injury time after Ospreys winger Vaughton got himself yellow-carded.

Half time score Gloucester 9 – 12 Ospreys

The breakthrough that Gloucester needed occurred three minutes into the second half. We turned over possession deep in the Ospreys half. Bucko picked out Allen who chose an inside line which put him clear of the defence. He had enough pace to beat Phillips to the line and he touched down for our first try of the day.

At Gloucester Rugby 14 – 12 Ospreys we went ahead for the first time in the match and Lamb extended our lead to Gloucester Rugby 16 – 12 Ospreys, when he knocked over the conversion.

With five minutes on the clock Delve replaced Qera and then Hook put his team a single point behind with a penalty three minutes later and with sixteen minutes on the clock he put his side in front once more with another penalty goal, putting the score at Gloucester Rugby 16 – 15 Ospreys. To add insult to injury Nieto was yellow-carded at the same time.

Chris Paterson replaced Lamb on seventeen minutes, just as Hook was landing another penalty to put his side in front again at Gloucester Rugby 16 – 18 Ospreys but two minutes later, with only fourteen players on the pitch we added our second try when Balshaw initiated an attack from a high kick from Hook.

Tindall supported on Balshaw's shoulder and when he took the pass he shipped it on to Simpson-Daniel who was cruising up with mischief in mind.

Sinbad slipped smoothly into warp factor five and the score was Gloucester Rugby 21 – 15 Ospreys. Paterson added the conversion and we were eight points clear at Gloucester Rugby 23 – 18 Ospreys as we went into the final twenty minutes of play. Califano came on for Strokosch and with twenty eight minutes of the half gone, Titterrell replaced Azam. Our big forwards played an immense part in keeping the ball away from the visitors as the game entered its final phase and we retained it for long periods, content to play the clock down and keep the Ospreys out of contention.

With thirty four minutes gone Paterson added another penalty and the match finished at Gloucester Rugby 26 – 18 Ospreys.

The positives for Gloucester were shutting the game down and preventing Ospreys getting a bonus point. It was a well-learned lesson we took to heart from our experience in playing Agen at Kingsholm last season. The negative aspect was the way in which we let them in for two soft first-half tries. But on the whole, the positives outweighed the negatives.

GLOUCESTER RUGBY	OSPREYS
Try: Allen, Paterson	**Try:** Parker (2)
Conversion: Lamb, Paterson	**Conversion:** Hook
Penalty Goal: Lamb (3), Paterson	**Penalty Goal:** Hook (2)

OTHER POOL 2 RESULT
Bourgoin 24 – 17 Ulster

Position	Club	Played	Points
1	Gloucester Rugby	2	9
2	Bourgoin	2	5
3	Ospreys	2	4
4	Ulster	2	2

Gloucester Rugby 27 – 25 Harlequins

Kick off 3.00pm Saturday 24 November 2007
Attendance 13,506 : D Rose referee

GLOUCESTER

15. O Morgan 14. J Simpson-Daniel 13. M Tindall 12. A Allen 11. L Vainikolo 10. C Paterson 9. G Cooper 1. P Collazo 2. A Titterrell 3. C Nieto 4. W James 5. M Bortolami 6. P Buxton 7. A Hazell 8. G Delve

Replacements
16. O Azam 17. A Dickinson 18. L Narraway 19. A Strokosch 20. R Lawson 21. R Lamb 22. I Balshaw

HARLEQUINS

15. M Brown 14. S Keogh 13. D Strettle 12. de W Barry 11. U Monye 10. C Malone 9. A Gomarsall 1. C Jones 2. T Fuga 3. M Ross 4. O Kohn 5. N Spanghero 6. C Robshaw   7. P Volley 8. N Easter

Replacements
16. C Brooker 17. R Nebbett 18. J Percival 19. W Skinner 20. S So'oialo 21. A Jarvis 22. J Turner-Hall

The lessons learned the previous week against the Ospreys clearly did not register as once more we had to work hard to dig ourselves out of a hole which we dug for ourselves.

The fact that we managed it and rescued four vital league points to boot, owed more to Big Les' finishing skills than a coherent game plan, though.

For the first half hour Harlequins – largely through the efforts of David Strettle aided and abetted by a marauding pack of forwards – rang rings round us.

Harlequins opened up their account at Gloucester Rugby 0 – 3 Harlequins with a Chris Malone penalty two minutes into the game and followed it up with a try by Keogh four minutes later. Strettle started the attack with a break through our defence and Barry and Robshaw arrived quickly to recycle the ball dangerously close to our line.

Ex-Gloucester player Andy Gomarsall whipped it quickly out to Keogh who crossed in the corner.

Malone missed the conversion from a wide position and the score stayed at

Gloucester Rugby 0 – 8 Harlequins.

With a quarter of an hour gone they added another unconverted try, this time through Monye, putting the score at Gloucester Rugby 0 – 13 Harlequins. The try followed another of Strettle's scything breaks; when the ball came back Malone dinked a little kick behind our defence and Monye was on it and scoring virtually before Gloucester had time to think.

Four minutes later Simpson-Daniel came inside from his wing and joined our attacking line. Hazey kept up the impetus before passing to Anthony Allen who put some real pace into the attack before shipping out a long pass to Lesley Vainikolo to score his first try for Gloucester at Kingsholm.

Paterson added the conversion to put us back in the match at Gloucester Rugby 7 – 13 Harlequins.

Five minutes later, with twenty four minutes on the clock, Andy Hazell got himself sin-binned for a so-called dangerous tackle on Monye and Harlequins wasted no time in taking advantage of their superior numbers, scoring a first-phase try through Malone three minutes later when he took a high pass from Gomarsall at the base of a scrum, threw an outrageous dummy outside and trotted in to score.

He had no trouble adding the conversion and the score stood at Gloucester Rugby 7 – 20 Harlequins.

Two minutes later Paterson kept us in touch at Gloucester 10 – 20 Harlequins with another penalty. But we were unable to stem the tide of Harlequins jerseys pouring into our half and eight minutes from the break they scored again when Keogh crossed our line to move the score on to Gloucester Rugby 10 – 25 Harlequins after Easter fed him on the blindside from a lineout drive.

Malone missed the conversion but all the same, fifteen points behind on your home ground is a pretty uncomfortable place to be. However Paterson managed to claw back three points when he knocked over another penalty to make the score slightly more respectable at Gloucester Rugby 13 – 25 Harlequins.

Half time score Gloucester Rugby 13 – 25 Harlequins

The Gloucester team which came out for the second half was far better-prepared than they had been in the first half. Harlequins were finding it difficult to cope with the Gloucester pack – one Gloucester rolling maul made thirty metres up the pitch – as the home side turned up the intensity.

It took a matter of four minutes for Gloucester to open their second half account. Morgan fielded the ball and launched a counter-attack from deep. Collazo got himself involved and kicked upfield. Paterson picked out Tindall who passed on to Allen before taking the return pass and touching down under the posts. Paterson added the conversion and at Gloucester Rugby 20 – 25 Harlequins, our show was back on the road again.

We made three quick substitutions: Azam replaced Titterrell, Narraway
came on for Will James, Rory Lawson substituted Gareth Cooper and Strokosch came on for Buxton.

The dynamic of the game changed when Gomarsall was yellow-carded on the fifty minute mark after Gloucester were prevented from having quick possession and three minutes later Harlequins loosehead Ceri Jones joined his scrumhalf in the sin bin for an infringement in the tackle area.

Harlequins defended valiantly but there is only so much a team of thirteen can achieve against a full complement and so it was inevitable that a try would be scored.

It came about from a ruck. Narraway linked with Big Les who came off his right foot like lightening and flew to the line for his second try of the day.

Paterson knocked over the conversion and the score was Gloucester 27 – 25 NEC Harlequins.

On the hour mark Lamb replaced Paterson and we seemed to spend the rest of the match tying up the opposition. In the entire half Harlequins were not awarded one single penalty, only a reversed decision, because of a Gloucester punch, went their way. Which forced a scathing post-match comment from their coach, Dean Richards.

Harlequins still had their moments though and spent long periods of time uncomfortably close to our try line but in the end Gloucester did enough to win the match.

GLOUCESTER RUGBY	HARLEQUINS
Try: Tindall, Vainikolo (2)	**Try:** Keogh (2), Malone, Monye
Conversion: Paterson (3)	**Conversion:** Malone
Penalty Goal: Paterson (2)	**Penalty Goal:** Malone

Worcester Warriors 15 – 34 Sale Sharks
Bath Rugby 28 – 13 Bristol Rugby
Leeds Carnegie 6 – 29 Leicester Tigers
London Wasps 35 – 12 Newcastle Falcons
Saracens 24 – 20 London Irish

CLUB	P	W	D	L	F	A	TF	TA	TB	LB	P
Gloucester Rugby	7	6	0	1	214	131	25	16	2	1	27
Bath Rugby	7	6	0	1	174	123	21	10	2	0	26
Saracens	7	5	0	2	192	153	20	14	1	2	23
Leicester Tigers	7	5	0	2	165	128	15	11	0	1	21
Harlequins	7	4	0	3	171	156	19	19	3	2	21
Sale Sharks	7	4	0	3	147	136	15	14	2	1	19
Bristol Rugby	7	3	0	4	126	138	12	12	1	1	14
Newcastle Falcons	7	3	0	4	121	153	14	18	1	1	14
London Wasps	7	2	1	4	148	141	15	13	1	2	13
London Irish	7	2	0	5	126	133	11	14	0	3	11
Leeds Carnegie	7	1	0	6	110	229	11	29	0	1	5
Worcester Warriors	7	0	1	6	118	191	13	21	0	2	4

Gwent Dragons 11 – 13 Gloucester Rugby

Kick off 7.30pm Friday 30 November 2007
Attendance 4,576 : D Richards (England) referee

GWENT DRAGONS

15. P Emerick 14. R Fussell 13. R Gomer Davies 12. G Maule 11. R Mustoe 10. C Sweeney 9. A Williams 1. A Black 2. B Daly 3. G Robinson 4. A Jones 5. P Sidoli 6. J Bearman 7. J Ringer 8. N Fitisemanu

Replacements

16. S Jones 17. H Gustafson 18. A Hall 19. L Evans 20. P Dollman 21. A Thomas 22. W Evans

GLOUCESTER RUGBY

15. O Morgan 14. J Bailey 13. L Lloyd 12. A James 11. M Foster 10. W Walker 9. M Prendergast 1. A Dickinson 2. J Paul 3. J Forster 4. W James 5. M Bortolami 6. A Strokosch 7. A Hazell 8. G Delve

Replacements

16. A Titterrell 17. C Califano 8. A Brown 19. L Narraway 20. G Cooper 21. C Paterson 22. J Simpson-Daniel

A Friday night match at Rodney Parade in an unrelenting monsoon; rugby does not come much more difficult than that but Gloucester faced it and pulled through to a satisfying conclusion... winning by all of two points after trailing the home side until the dying seconds of the match.

We opened the scoring with a Willie Walker penalty after four minutes to put us in the lead at Gwent Dragons 0 – 3 Gloucester Rugby but Ceri Sweeney drew level after seventeen minutes with a penalty for the home side.

With thirty six minutes on the clock Alex Brown replaced the injured Marco Bortolami and then on the forty minute mark Dragons scored a try to take the lead at Gwent Dragons 8 – 3 Gloucester Rugby. It happened when Sweeney kicked through and the follow up was so fast that Mike Prendergast was left with no option but to kick the ball dead.

From the ensuing scrum – one of the few of the evening which did not collapse – the home team kept possession long enough to drive loosehead Adam Black over the line to touch down.

Sweeney's conversion attempt failed and they went in for a well-deserved cup of tea and fresh jerseys at Gwent Dragons 0 – 3 Gloucester Rugby.

Half time score Gwent Dragons 8 - 3 Gloucester Rugby

Six minutes into the second half Willie Walker slotted a penalty when Dragons were adjudged offside after a run by Hazell and Jeremy Paul, who by his own admission had never experienced weather conditions like it before. The kick put us closer at Gwent Dragons 8 – 6 Gloucester Rugby then four minutes later Christian Califano came on for Dickinson.

And so the game continued with Gloucester having the lion's share of possession but being unable to capitalise on it.

Then with an hour gone, Emerick followed up a Williams kick, Foster's clearance was charged down and Gloucester were penalised for killing the ball. Sweeney stretched the home side's lead to Gwent Dragons 11 – 6 Gloucester Rugby when he landed his second penalty of the day.

At this point in the match Narraway replaced Strokosch and Cooper came on for Prendergast. A few minutes later Titterrell came on for Jeremy Paul and Paterson replaced Morgan and with only two minutes of ordinary time left Sinbad replaced Andy Hazell. Then one minute later Morgan replaced Ali James.

The game looked to be all over for us until, dead on time, Ollie Morgan managed a break down the left, Bailey appeared on his outside shoulder and when he got the pass kicked it behind Emerick.

Sweeney gathered the ball and shaped up to kick it out of trouble but Will James was up like an express train and charged it down. A scrum ensued and Gareth Delve was driven over to touch down close to the posts, putting the score level at Gwent Dragons 11 – 11 Gloucester Rugby.

Chris Paterson made no mistake with his conversion and we were in front at Gwent Dragons 11 – 13 Gloucester Rugby. Injury time lasted three minutes and Gloucester played cleverly to retain possession and run the clock down with a series of rucks and short range attacks.

GWENT DRAGONS	GLOUCESTER RUGBY
Try: Black	**Try:** Delve
Penalty Goal: Sweeney (2)	**Conversion:** Paterson
	Penalty Goal: Walker (2)

OTHER POOL A RESULT
London Wasps 24 – 6 Newcastle Falcons

Position	Club	Played	Points
1	London Wasps	3	11
2	Gloucester Rugby	3	8
3	Newcastle Falcons	3	7
4	Gwent Dragons	3	5

Stade Pierre Rajon

Bourgoin 7 – 31 Gloucester Rugby
Kick off 9.00pm Friday 7 December 2007
Attendance 6,500 : A Rolland (Ireland) referee

BOURGOIN

15. A Forest 14. D Janin 13. R Coetzee 12. S Laloo 11. M Nicolas 10. B Boyet 9. M Parra 1. Ka Wihongi 2. B Cabello 3. P Cardinali 4. J Pierre 5. D Fevre 6. J Frier 7. M Rennie 8. W Jooste

Replacements

16. J-P Genevois 17. O Sourgens 18. C Wyatt 19. S Nicolas 20. M Forest 21. M Viazzo 22. J-F Coux

GLOUCESTER RUGBY

15. O Morgan 14. J Simpson-Daniel 13. M Tindall 12. A Allen 11. I Balshaw 10. R Lamb 9. R Lawson 1. N Wood 2. O Azam 3. C Nieto 4. P Buxton 5. A Brown 6. A Strokosch 7. A Qera 8. G Delve

Replacements

16. A Titterrell 17. C Califano 18. W James 19. L Narraway 20. G Cooper 21. C Paterson 22. L Lloyd

Gloucester put on a thoroughly creditable performance at the Stade Pierre Rajon, culminating in a bonus point earned in the last play of the match for an away victory that was to stand us in good stead. Whereas our opening European Cup Pool 2 matches against Ulster and the Ospreys were characterised by ferocity and determination, this match displayed our ability to exert the three c's: control, composure and concentration.

Bourgoin also exhibited three c's which were more than slightly different to ours: a high error count in the contact area which cost 'em dearly.

We got the best of all possible starts, scoring from first phase possession after five minutes play when we won a scrum and Lamb got the ball to Anthony Allen who swerved and rolled out of a couple of tackles to touch down. At Bourgoin 0 – 5 Gloucester Rugby, Lamb added the conversion and our lead moved on to seven points without reply.

We quickly established our superiority in most areas of play and we pinned the home side in their own half for long stretches of play and when Nick Wood put the squeeze on their loosehead Cardinali we were awarded a penalty which Lamby had no hesitation in converting into three more points. Bourgoin 0 – 10 Gloucester Rugby with twenty two minutes gone.

Twelve minutes later Gloucester drove infield from a lineout and Lamb

made a half-break inside before some exquisite handling which put the ball in Simpson-Daniel's hands as he chose an inside line in a move reminiscent of Philippe Saint-Andre. He touched down unchallenged near the posts and Lamby added the conversion to put the score at Bourgoin 0 – 17 Gloucester Rugby.

Sinbad was presented with another scoring chance when Tindall kicked and chased and made his own tackle. Balshaw moved it on and when it came back to Lamby he dinked the ball through for Sinbad who made an uncharacteristic handling error. Being seventeen points to nil up at half time in a European Cup match is like all your Christmases coming at once and the Gloucester Boys went in for the break justifiably elated with their performance.

Half time score Bourgoin 0 – 17 Gloucester Rugby

Eight minutes into the second half Lamby converted his own try which came from an interception. He took his opposite number's pass near the halfway line and fled the fifty metres to touch down near the posts to make his conversion attempt even easier. With the kick the score moved on to Bourgoin 0 – 24 Gloucester Rugby.

We made three quick injury replacements in a matter of about four minutes. Lloyd came on for Ollie Morgan; Titterrell replaced Azam and Paterson came on for Tindall.

It was at this point that the weather deteriorated into an all out thunderstorm, complete with dramatic lightening flashes.

The change in the weather heralded a temporary change in the order of the game and Bourgoin staged a recovery of sorts. After a series of determined tries they finally crossed our line through a try from a ruck by their blindside flanker Frier after fifty nine minutes and Boyet added the conversion to move the score on to Bourgoin 7 – 24 Gloucester Rugby.

But no matter how determined the French attacks, they were continually repelled by an equally-determined Gloucester defence.

On the hour mark Iain Balshaw was replaced on the wing by Gareth Cooper and one minute later Narraway replaced Strokosch. Three minutes later Balshaw was back on as a substitute for Chris Paterson and so the match progressed.

In the eightieth minute Lamb picked out Narraway coming on the burst through the centre and the first line of defence was breached. Narraway made the scoring pass to Titterrell who touched down for Lamb to add the conversion and close the match at Bourgoin 7 – 31 Gloucester Rugby.

The problems with our scrummage seemed to have been eradicated and out of a possible fifteen pool points Gloucester had bagged fourteen and we were justifiably proud having produced a memorable – even a vintage - performance against confident opponents under the direst weather conditions.

As you would expect, there was a downside to the match. Three of our players, in the shape of Morgan, Paterson and Tindall were injured and the loss of any one of them could prove costly to the Gloucester cause.

BOURGOIN	GLOUCESTER RUGBY
Try: Frier	**Try:** Allen, Lamb, S-Daniel, Titterrell
Conversion: Boyet	**Conversion:** Lamb (4)
	Penalty Goal: Lamb

OTHER POOL 2 RESULT
Ospreys 48 – 17 Ulster

Position	Club	Played	Points
1	Gloucester Rugby	3	14
2	Ospreys	3	9
3	Bourgoin	3	5
4	Ulster	3	1

Kingsholm
Gloucester Rugby 51 – 27 Bourgoin
kick off 3.00pm Saturday 15 December 2007
Attendance 12,370 : G Clancy (Ireland) referee

GLOUCESTER

15. I Balshaw 14. J Simpson-Daniel 13. M Tindall 12. A Allen
11. L Vainikolo 10. R Lamb 9. R Lawson 1. N Wood 2. O
Azam 3. C Nieto 4. P Buxton 5. A Brown 6. L Narraway 7. A
Qera 8. G Delve

Replacements
16. A Titterrell 17. C Califano 18. M Bortolami 19. A Strokosch
20. G Cooper 21. W Walker 22. L Lloyd

BOURGOIN

15. F Denos 14. M Nicolas 13. R Coetzee 12. M Viazzo 11. D
Janin 10. B Boyet 9. M Parra 1. A T Kamga 2. J-P Genevois
3. O Sourgens 4. C Wyatt 5. D Fevre   6. B Monzeglio 7. M
Rennie 8. W Jooste

Replacements
16. B Cabello 17. K Wihongi 18. J Pierre 19. A Petrilli   20. R
Mandon 21. N Carmona 22. A Forest

The game started as you would expect, with both sides trying
to build a score. Lamb slotted a penalty in the first minute
(Gloucester Rugby 3 – 0 Bourgoin) and two minutes later
Boyet replied with the visitors' first penalty and the score was
level at Gloucester Rugby 3 – 3 Bourgoin.

With six minutes gone Lamb scored our second penalty
(Gloucester Rugby 6 – 3 Bourgoin) and eight minutes later
Bourgoin drew level with their second penalty, courtesy of
Boyet: Gloucester Rugby 6 – 6 Bourgoin.

With sixteen minutes ticked off the clock Lamb neatly slotted
our third penalty to put us in the lead again at Gloucester
Rugby 9 – 6 Bourgoin.

Then, as the first quarter of the match was drawing to a close
we opened up a more convincing lead with a well-worked try.
Simpson-Daniel fielded a kick ahead and fixed his opponent
with a run at his inside shoulder. Balshaw came into the line

and called for the ball then shifted it on to Qera who moved it on to Tindall.

Tindall kicked through and Qera followed up to pounce on the ball for our first try of the day and moved the score on to Gloucester Rugby 14 – 6 Bourgoin.

Lamb added the conversion and we were ten points clear at Gloucester Rugby 16 – 6 Bourgoin.

Three minutes later we started to put clear blue water between us and our visitors when we ran in our second try. We were awarded a free kick at a scrum and Delve took it up. The ball came back and Simpson-Daniel and Luke Narraway moved it forward into the shadow of the goalposts. Then the ball came left and Big Les executed an inside pass to Tindall. At the tackle area near the Bourgoin line Gareth Delve finished off the move he started and found a way over to put us fifteen points clear at Gloucester Rugby 21 – 6 Bourgoin.

Lamb, who was having a massive game, knocked over the conversion and the score was Gloucester Rugby 23 – 6 Bourgoin.

Again Gloucester were putting on a display of controlled and confident rugby so it was ironic in the extreme that an uncharacteristic Gloucester mistake led to Bourgoin's first try when they were a man down, their lock Fevre having been yellow carded on twenty five minutes play.

With thirty two minutes on the clock we attempted to play from a deep position and lost the ball in contact. It was scooped up by Rennie the openside who sent Nicolas the winger over with an inside pass. He ran behind the posts to make the conversion easier for Boyet who duly obliged and moved the score on to Gloucester Rugby 23 – 13 Bourgoin.

With the French team getting back to within ten points of us there was a slightly uncomfortable, nervy feeling around the ground at our inability to add points while our opponents were reduced to fourteen players but all misgivings were put to rest three minutes from half time when we took a quick lineout and got behind their defence courtesy of Tindall and Narraway. The ball came back and Lamb shifted it to Qera who took it into contact at pace.

From the ensuing ruck a classic backs move put Balshaw over to move the score on to Gloucester Rugby 28 – 13 Bourgoin when he came into the line to end a straightforward handling move from Lawson, Lamb and Allen.

Once more Lamb added a confident conversion and the score was Gloucester Rugby 30 – 13 Bourgoin. That is how the half ended. With forty three points scored, the scoreboard operator probably needed a sit down and a cup of tea every bit as much as the players.

Half time score Gloucester Rugby 30 – 13 Bourgoin

The whistle went and it was time for some more of the same. Walker was substituted for Balshaw and six minutes into the half Narraway and Delve made inroads into the French defence. The ball came back and Lamb passed it to Walker who swerved and sidestepped his way behind the line and ran behind the posts to touch down try number four. Lamb converted and it was Gloucester Rugby 37 – 13 Bourgoin.

With fifty four minutes gone Bortolami replaced Narraway and seven minutes after we scored our fifth try. There were shades of *déjà vu* when Boyet chose a flat line in the middle of the pitch across our defence looking to send out a long pass. Lamby read it, reached it and ran it in from fifty-odd metres in an action replay of his try in France the previous week. He added the conversion to his own try and with the score at Gloucester Rugby 44 – 13 Bourgoin, there were unconfirmed rumours that the bloke operating the scorebaord was suffering from exhaustion and had to be substituted...

One minute past the hour mark we made three substitutions: Titterrell came on for Azam, Califano came on for Nieto and Cooper replaced Lawson.

Four minutes later Bourgoin scored a try through hooker Jean-Philippe Genevois who was driven over after a succession of driving mauls. At Gloucester Rugby 44 – 18 Bourgoin, Boyet knocked over the conversion and the score stood at Gloucester Rugby 44 – 20 Bourgoin.

But there was still more to come. Ten minutes from time the Gloucester forwards drove into the Bourgoin defence and Sinbad headed for the line at pace. He shipped it out to Big Les who erupted from short range and touched down for another Gloucester try. Lamb made the conversion and our score moved on past the half-century mark at Gloucester 51 – 18 Bourgoin. At this point Strokosch came on for Buxton and Leon Lloyd replaced Tindall.

However it was Bourgoin who scored the final points of the game when on seventy nine minutes their flanker Monzeglio touched down from close range. Boyet converted and the final score was Gloucester Rugby 51 – 27 Bourgoin.

The win gave us a huge cushion of nineteen Pool points at the top of Pool Two and the six tries gave the players enormous confidence. Lamb's personal contribution of twenty six points earned him the man of the match award for the third time in four matches. Why not? With a tally of nine goal kicks from nine attempts his record for the afternoon was perfect and he was aided and abetted by a glorious all-round team performance. It was a great afternoon's sport.

GLOUCESTER RUGBY	BOURGOIN
Try: Balshaw, Delve, Lamb, Qera, Vainikoko, Walker	**Try:** Genevois, Monzeglio, Nicolas
Conversion: Lamb (6)	**Conversion:** Boyet (3)
Penalty Goal: Lamb (3)	**Penalty Goal:** Boyet (2)

OTHER POOL 2 RESULT
Ulster 8 – 16 Ospreys

Position	Club	Played	Points
1	Gloucester Rugby	4	19
2	Ospreys	4	13
3	Bourgoin	4	5
4	Ulster	4	1

Newcastle Falcons 13 – 20 Gloucester Rugby

Kick off 3.00pm Sunday 23 December 2007
Attendance 9,612 : M Fox referee

NEWCASTLE FALCONS

15. M Tait 14. T May 13. J Noon 12. T Flood 11. J Rudd 10. J Wilkinson 9. L Dickson 1. J Golding 2. A Long 3. C Hayman 4. A Perry 5. M Sorenson 6. G Parling 7. B Woods 8. R Winter

Replacements

16. R Vickers 17. D Wilson 18. S Tomes 19. B Wilson 20. J Grindal 21. T Visser 22. O Phillips

GLOUCESTER RUGBY

15. I Balshaw 14. J Simpson-Daniel 13. M Tindall 12. A Allen 11. L Vainikolo 10. R Lamb 9. G Cooper 1. N Wood 2. O Azam 3. C Nieto 4. M Bortolami 5. A Brown 6. A Strokosch 7. L Narraway 8. G Delve

Replacements

16. A Titterrell 17. P Collazo 18. W James 19. P Buxton 20. R Lawson 21. W Walker 22. L Lloyd

A defeat of Newcastle in their own back yard is a good enough Christmas present for any self-respecting Gloucester supporter, irrespective of whether they actually made the extended trip to the frozen north for this Sunday afternoon match.

The question marks against our scrummage were deleted several weeks ago and it gave us the platform we needed to keep our position at the top of the league even though they were sporting All Black tighthead legend Carl Hayman to scrummaging against Nick Wood.

Wilkinson opened the scoring for his side with a six-minute penalty when we were blown up for off side but two minutes later we scored our first try when Gareth Delve prised open the first line of defence. Cooper took it on with an artful half break and Tindall drove mercilessly towards the line.

When the ball came back Bortolami improvised with an overhead pass to get the ball out to Balshaw who rewarded the move with a try which Lamb promptly converted from the touchline and the score was Newcastle Falcons 3 – 7 Gloucester Rugby.

On twenty two minutes Parling responded with a Newcastle try after Oli Azam locked horns with Hayman on the ground. Dickson threw it out to Winter on the blindside and Parling took it over our line to put his side back in the lead at Newcastle Falcons 8 – 7 Gloucester Rugby. Wilkinson made no mistake with the conversion and moved his side into a three point lead at Newcastle Falcons 10 – 7 Gloucester Rugby.

Newcastle openside Woods was yellow carded at twenty seven minutes for a deliberate knock on when he intercepted a Gloucester pass. We kicked for the corner but Azam overcooked his throw and a scoring chance went begging but four minutes later we took full advantage of the extra man to score our second try.

Lamb kicked a penalty to touch and we prepared for the catch-and-drive. Delve took it at the tail of the lineout and Oli Azam was bundled over to claim the try and earn absolution for his earlier cock up. At Newcastle Falcons 10 – 12 Gloucester Rugby Lamb scored the conversion and we went in for the break at Newcastle Falcons 10 – 14 Gloucester Rugby.

Half time score Newcastle Falcons 10 – 14 Gloucester Rugby

With forty five minutes gone we substituted Lawson for Cooper and six minutes later Buxton came on for Delve and with thirteen minutes of the second half gone Newcastle were penalised for off-side and Lamb slotted the kick to put us nicely in the clear by seven points at Newcastle Falcons 10 – 17 Gloucester Rugby. Ten minutes later Titterrell replaced Azam.

We made a hash of several scoring chances, but then, so did Newcastle. But our chances were spoiled by handling errors once we had crossed the gainline whereas the home side was unable to get behind the Gloucester defence for a period of sufficient length to cause us any real problems.

However Wilkinson did slam over a penalty ten minutes from the end to make the score Newcastle Falcons 13 – 17 Gloucester Rugby.

Will James came on for Marco Bortolami and with seven minutes of the match remaining Lamb knocked over another penalty when Newcastle were penalised for entering a ruck from the side.

At Newcastle Falcons 13 – 20 Gloucester Rugby the home side were left needing a converted try to draw the match and it was beyond them.

NEWCASTLE FALCONS	GLOUCESTER RUGBY
Try: Parling	**Try:** Azam, Balshaw
Conversion: Wilkinson	**Conversion:** Lamb (2)
Penalty Goal: Wilkinson (2)	**Penalty Goal:** Lamb (2)

OTHER RESULTS

Bath Rugby 20 – 3 Leeds Carnegie
Bristol Rugby 23 – 23 London Wasps
Harlequins 20 – 27 Saracens
Sale Sharks 20 – 14 Leicester Tigers
London Irish 23 – 16 Worcester Warriors

CLUB	P	W	D	L	F	A	TF	TA	TB	LB	P
Gloucester Rugby	8	7	0	1	234	144	27	17	2	1	31
Bath Rugby	8	7	0	1	215	133	26	11	3	0	31
Saracens	8	6	0	2	219	173	23	16	1	2	27
Sale Sharks	8	5	0	3	167	150	16	15	2	1	23
Leicester Tigers	8	5	0	3	179	148	16	12	0	2	22
Harlequins	8	4	0	4	191	183	21	22	3	3	22
Bristol Rugby	8	3	1	4	149	161	15	14	1	1	16
London Irish	8	3	0	5	149	149	13	15	0	3	15
Newcastle Falcons	8	3	0	5	134	173	15	20	1	2	15
London Wasps	8	2	2	4	171	164	17	16	1	2	15
Leeds Carnegie	8	1	0	7	120	270	12	34	0	1	5
Worcester Warriors	8	0	1	7	134	214	14	23	0	3	5

Gloucester Rugby 27 – 0 Bristol Rugby

Kick off 3.00pm Saturday 29 December 2007
Attendance 16,500 : D Pearson referee

GLOUCESTER RUGBY

15. W Walker 14. J Simpson-Daniel 13. M Tindall 12. A Allen 11. L Vainikolo 10. R Lamb 9. R Lawson 1. N Wood 2. O Azam 3. C Califano 4. M Bortolami 5. A Brown 6. A Strokosch 7. A Qera 8. L Narraway

Replacements

16. J Paul 17. J Forster 18. W James 19. P Buxton 20. M Prendergast 21. C Paterson 22. L Lloyd

BRISTOL RUGBY

15. L Arscott 14. T Arscott 13. R Higgitt 12. S Cox 11. D Lemi 10. D Hill 9. B O'Riordan 1. A Clarke 2. S Linklater 3. D Crompton 4. R Winters 5. S Hohneck 6. M Salter 7. A T Vaeluaga 8. A Blowers

Replacements

16. M Regan 17. D Hilton 18. D Attwood 19. J El Abd 20. H Thomas 21. E Barnes 22. A Elliott

Ryan Lamb opened the scoresheet with a penalty after four minutes and ten minutes later Leon Lloyd was brought on to replace Tindall who limped off with a calf injury.

Three minutes later we crossed the Bristol line for our first try courtesy of Olivier Azam who pounced from a lineout. Lamb missed with his conversion attempt and the score stayed at Gloucester Rugby 8 – 0 Bristol Rugby.

Just before the half hour mark we scored another try, this time through Leon Lloyd after Bristol lost possession in the midfield. Simpson-Daniel and Big Les combined to take it deep into Bristol territory and when it came back Lamb put in a perfectly-weighted cross kick which Lloyd caught in flight and fled to the opposition line. This time Lamb's conversion attempt was successful and he moved the score on to Gloucester Rugby 15 – 0 Bristol Rugby.

Half time score Gloucester Rugby 15 – 0 Bristol Rugby

The second half continued in much the same vein with the Gloucester pack
in control and the bonus point looking a very strong possibility.
The catalyst for the second half seemed to be when Strokosch replaced Buxton on fifty nine minutes. One minute later Azam adopted the role of decision-maker, taking a tap penalty and charging upfield before offloading to Willie Walker who had come into the line from the fullback position. Support runners were queuing up outside Walker and he threw out a long pass to Simpson-Daniel who put some pace into the attack as only he can. With Big Les steaming up in support Sinbad wrong-footed the last defender with a dummy to the big man and scored in the corner, taking the score to Gloucester Rugby 20 - 0 Bristol Rugby. The game-over lights were starting to flash at the back of Bristol minds by this time, even though Lamby missed the conversion. However he made up for it six minutes later when Leon Lloyd crossed the Bristol line in the sixty sixth minute.
Again it was created by Azam who made the hard yards with several Bristol defenders collectively attempting to dissuade him from this course of action. Bucko took it on and Lawson appeared at his shoulder to take the pass, moving it on to Lloydy who had space to move and from there he scored his second try of the day, taking the score to Gloucester Rugby 25 – 0 Bristol Rugby. There was no mistake over Lamb's conversion and at Gloucester Rugby 27 – 0 Bristol Rugby with fourteen minutes to go Dave Pearson might just as well have blown his whistle there and then but the laws of rugby preclude an early finish to prevent further injury and so Bristol were allowed to stagger on.
With eleven minutes to go Matt Salter was sinbinned for fouling Vainikolo at the side of a ruck and Gloucester made a couple of substitutions: Paterson for Allen on sixty nine minutes; Forster for Califano and Will James for Alex Brown, both on seventy one minutes.
With five minutes of ordinary time to go Marco Bortolami was yellow carded for a lineout offence and with three minutes to go we made two more substitutions – Prendergast for Lawson and Jeremy Paul for Azam.

That Gloucester is capable of the basics of attack and defence is a given; but some new skills were on display for the Gloucester support to admire, too. They showed an ability to regroup and reorganise after injuries changed the complexion of their game. And most notably they showed a sort of professional ruthlessness to take advantage of the opportunities which happened along.

A perfectionist would say that Gloucester are capable of a higher quality of rugby than this exhibition displayed but a derby win is a derby win and it put connections in the right frame of mind for the following weekend's league match derby at Bath's Recreation Ground...

GLOUCESTER RUGBY
Try: Azam, Lloyd (2), S-Daniel
Conversion: Lamb (2)
Penalty Goal: Lamb

OTHER RESULTS
Leicester Tigers 25 - 17 London Irish
London Wasps 25 - 10 Bath Rugby
Worcester Warriors 7 – 10 Harlequins
Leeds Carnegie 20 - 34 Sale Sharks
Saracens 19 - 22 Newcastle Falcons

CLUB	P	W	D	L	F	A	TF	TA	TB	LB	P
Gloucester Rugby	9	8	0	1	261	144	31	17	3	1	36
Bath Rugby	9	7	0	2	225	158	27	14	3	0	31
Saracens	9	6	0	3	238	195	25	19	1	3	28
Sale Sharks	9	6	0	3	201	170	20	18	3	1	28
Leicester Tigers	9	6	0	3	204	165	20	13	1	2	27
Harlequins	9	5	0	4	201	190	23	23	3	3	26
Newcastle Falcons	9	4	0	5	156	192	18	22	1	2	19
London Wasps	9	3	2	4	196	174	20	17	1	2	19
Bristol Rugby	9	3	1	5	149	188	15	18	1	1	16
London Irish	9	3	0	6	166	174	14	19	0	3	15
Worcester Warriors	9	0	1	8	141	224	15	25	0	4	6
Leeds Carnegie	9	1	0	8	140	304	15	38	0	1	5

Guinness Premiership
Round Ten
Recreation Ground

Bath Rugby 10 – 5 Gloucester Rugby

Kick off 8.00pm Friday 4 January 2008
Attendance 10,600 : W Barnes referee

BATH RUGBY
15. N Abendanon 14. J Maddock 13. A Crockett 12. O Barkley 11. M Banahan 10. A James 9. M Claassens 1. D Barnes 2. L Mears 3. M Stevens 4. S Borthwick 5. D Grewcock 6. A Beattie 7. M Lipman 8. D Browne

Replacements
16. P Dixon 17. P Ion 18. P Short 19. J Fa'amatuainu 20. N Walshe 21. S Berne 22. M Stephenson

GLOUCESTER RUGBY
15. W Walker 14. L Lloyd 13. M Tindall 12. A Allen 11. J Bailey 10. R Lamb 9. R Lawson 1. N Wood 2. O Azam 3. C Nieto 4. M Bortolami 5. A Brown 6. P Buxton 7. A Qera 8. L Narraway

Replacements
16. J Paul 17. P Collazo 18. W James 19. A Strokosch 20. M Prendergast 21. C Paterson 22. M Foster

An away match at Bath. What a way to celebrate a New Year! Coming off the back of a consummate whipping of Bristol the previous week, Gloucester tails were up and there was a collective belief that 2008 would be the year when we finally put Bath to the sword in a league match in their own back yard.

At 8.00pm the Friday night kick off was nice and late to allow stragglers and travellers to make their way to the ground. And so the stage was set for Gloucester to wash away seventeen years of hurt... or was it?

Well, frankly no, it wasn't! Well, we did emerge with a losing bonus point so the night was not a complete shambles but it was a miserable evening weather-wise and an away win for us would have been gratefully accepted – but there you are. You

137

can't have everything. Especially when you are talking about derby matches.

There was more water on the pitch than in the nearby River Avon after hours of monsoon-like rain which was sure to favour the home side. A point which cheered them no end but seriously dampened the spirits of the visiting Gloucester supporters.

When a Premiership match ends with a scoreline like an American basketball game, the greybeards among the Gloucester support say they would rather witness a Bath versus Gloucester match that resulted in a six points to three result, which went either way. Provided the penalties were all fairly awarded and the game was played in an honourable fashion. Although not quite six points to three, this match came close to fulfilling these requirements and although bitterly disappointed, Gloucester have no axe to grind about the result.

Anyway, the stage was set with both sides fancying their chances with a successful form line through Bristol Rugby. In round seven of the Premiership, Bath had defeated their next door neighbours 28 – 13 and in round nine we had defeated them 27 – 0.

Gloucester's confidence took a knock over the weather conditions. The kick off was delayed for fifteen minutes while referee Wayne Barnes discussed the wisdom of the match going ahead with the two captains. Bath were keen to go ahead, sensing they would have the advantage under the conditions and Gloucester would obviously have preferred an adjournment until better conditions prevailed where our lighter more mobile team would have then had the advantage.

Perhaps it is my cynical side which says that if the Sky TV cameras had not been present the game would have been called off or perhaps it is the bad loser in me blaming the referee for allowing the match to go ahead.

Whatever the underlying reasons we were treated to a far better game than anyone had a right to expect, considering the conditions.

It is not easy to write this, but Bath were awesome. Their forwards were on the top of their game and their backs played some stupendous football, having regard to the conditions. Meanwhile we showed them some proper old-fashioned Gloucester dog with an heroic display of defending.

Time and again the Bath forwards drove relentlessly at the fringes and time and again Gloucester stoically defended the gainline as if far more was at stake than a handful of league points.

That is one of the supreme ironies of the sporting contest. The fact that men will risk everything – their health, their livelihood, their wellbeing, their lives even – for something as trivial and meaningless as possession of a ball and points in a league table.

The other great irony is that supporters like you and me acknowledge the meaninglessness of it all and yet still we harbour a compulsion to be a party to it. To witness the drama unfold. To glorify it. To embellish it in the telling.

It took over half an hour for Bath to find a way to break and enter our defences and then it was as much our responsibility as theirs according to the ref.

On the thirty two minute mark barrister-referee Barnes found Marco Bortolami guilty of lazy running. Lazy running indeed. We should all have accounted ourselves lucky that any of the players were still capable of running at all under the conditions and with due deference to the amount of energy already expended.

Barkley sent his kick through the posts and there was finally a figure on the scoreboard: Bath Rugby 3 – 0 Gloucester. The remaining ten minutes of the half were played out much the same as the first half hour.

Half time score Bath Rugby 3 – 0 Gloucester Rugby

Ten minutes into the second half they found their way to our try line. It followed a period of unswerving defence against a series of rucks and when we finally got possession Oli Azam kicked it long and clear but Abendanon put a kick over the top of Bailey for Maddock to chase and slide over the line. Barkley added the conversion and the score was Bath Rugby 10 – 0 Gloucester Rugby.

Three minutes later we made three substitutions in the hope that we might be able to recapture our ability to move around the pitch and get some possession with which we could launch an attack. Paul came on for Azam, Collazo substituted Wood and Strokosch replaced Bortolami.

With fifty nine minutes gone Paterson replaced Ryan Lamb. And one minute later the ball came out to Paterson. He stood in the middle of the pitch in a jersey so clean that it looked as if there was a spotlight on him, or he was in a Daz advert or he was an angel or something. So pure and clean was he in comparison to the twenty nine other muddied and bedraggled blokes out there (thirty, if you include the ref).

For an hour of unremitting slog the blokes in Gloucester jerseys had nearly killed themselves just to get their hands on the ball and suddenly – irony of ironies – Paterson had it and with his first touch he skipped around Shaun Berne and covered the intervening fifty metres to score a try as he pleased, moving the score to Bath Rugby 10 – 5 Gloucester Rugby.

Watching this drama unfold before our very eyes our little clique burst into spontaneous childish laughter. Laughter at the relief of scoring a try at long last. Laughter because we could imagine what was going through the minds of the other Gloucester players. Laughter because we knew we were going to lose and it didn't really matter because our team had done all they could. Laughter just because sometimes it can be the greatest fun in the world to support Gloucester even in the pouring rain at the Recreation Ground when you are on a hiding to nothing.

This was the point which could have swung the match in our favour but we knew it was not going to happen. Paterson missed the conversion and the game reverted to its earlier pattern – Bath attacked and Gloucester defended.

Fifteen minutes from the end Will James replaced Qera and the game went on with no further score.

The result cut our league lead to two points but we were still top and Bath are still second and there is always our last home Premiership match on 10 May to look forward to. When we take on Bath at Kingsholm to seek revenge and give us bragging rights through the summer break.

Things could be worse.

BATH RUGBY
Try: Maddock
Conversion: Barkley
Penalty Goal: Barkley

GLOUCESTER RUGBY
Try: Paterson

OTHER RESULTS
London Wasps 25 - 17 Leeds Carnegie
Harlequins 13 - 42 Leicester Tigers
Bristol Rugby 18 - 3 Saracens
London Irish 20 - 12 Sale Sharks
Newcastle Falcons 15 - 12 Worcester Warriors

CLUB	P	W	D	L	F	A	TF	TA	TB	LB	P
Gloucester Rugby	10	8	0	2	266	154	32	18	3	2	37
Bath Rugby	10	8	0	2	235	163	28	15	3	0	35
Leicester Tigers	10	7	0	3	246	178	25	14	2	2	32
Saracens	10	6	0	4	241	213	25	21	1	3	28
Sale Sharks	10	6	0	4	213	190	20	21	3	1	28
Harlequins	10	5	0	5	214	232	24	28	3	3	26
Newcastle Falcons	10	5	0	5	171	204	18	24	1	2	23
London Wasps	10	4	2	4	221	191	23	19	1	2	23
Bristol Rugby	10	4	1	5	167	191	17	18	1	1	20
London Irish	10	4	0	6	186	186	17	19	0	3	19
Worcester Warriors	10	0	1	9	153	239	17	25	0	5	7
Leeds Carnegie	10	1	0	9	157	329	17	41	0	1	5

Heineken Cup Pool Two
Liberty Stadium

Ospreys 32 - 15 Gloucester Rugby

kick off 5.30pm Saturday 12 January 2008
Attendance 18,017 : A Lewis (Ireland) referee

OSPREYS

15. L Byrne 14. N Walker 13. S Parker 12. G Henson 11. S
Williams 10. J Hook 9. J Marshall 1. D Jones 2. H Bennett 3. A
Jones 4. I Gough 5. A-W Jones 6. R Jones 7. M Holah 8. F
Tiatia

Replacements

16. R Hibbard 17. P James 18. I Evans 19. J Thomas 20. M
Phillips 21. M Taylor 22. J Vaughton

GLOUCESTER RUGBY

15. I Balshaw 14. J Simpson-Daniel 13. M Tindall 12. A Allen
11. L Lloyd 10. R Lamb 9. G Cooper 1. C Califano 2. A
Titterrell 3. C Nieto 4. M Bortolami 5. A Brown 6. P Buxton 7.
A Qera 8. G Delve

Replacements

16. O Azam 17. P Collazo 18. A Strokosch 19. L Narraway 20.
R Lawson 21. C Paterson 22. W Walker

Another rainy night another Gloucester defeat. The time was
when driving rain and a muddy pitch provided the basics for
any decent Gloucester victory. How things change.
We went three points behind five minutes into the match and
that set the tone for the evening.
Six minutes later Henson gathered an inaccurate pass from
his stand off James Hook and hoisted a towering garryowen
and three Gloucester players, alphabetically Balshaw, Cooper
and Lloyd did the rabbit-in-the-headlights trick, standing stock-
still while the ball bounced without making any attempt to deal
with it, although Balshaw had the composure to cover and
make the tackle, inches from the line, on Henson who had
come through, jumped to get possession and then run the
length of the Gloucester twenty two.
From the ensuing ruck Shane Williams crossed our line and
Hook converted. In a heartbeat we went ten points behind at
Ospreys 10 – 0 Gloucester Rugby.

142

Things were starting to look uncomfortable for us and the misery worsened when Alex Brown went off injured and was replaced by Will James.

With eighteen minutes of the half gone Hook knocked over another penalty to put the score at Ospreys 13 – 0 Gloucester Rugby, but Gloucester finally made it on to the scoreboard with twenty six minutes gone when Lamb slotted his first penalty, putting the score at Ospreys 13 – 3 Gloucester Rugby but Hook still managed another brace of penalties on twenty seven and thirty six minutes to put his side sixteen points clear at Ospreys 19 – 3 Gloucester Rugby.

The second of these resulted in a yellow card for Buxton when he supposedly creamed Justin Marshall at a ruck but the Gloucester support believed – by and large – that Marshall took a dive.

Half time score Ospreys 19- 3 Gloucester Rugby

At the start of the second half Azam replaced Titterrell and Paterson came on for Lloyd but we could not stem the haemorrhage of points. After fifty two minutes Hook landed another penalty and moved his team on to a nineteen points lead at Ospreys 22 – 3 Gloucester Rugby. We substituted Cooper with Lawson one minute later. Inspired tactics from Dean Ryan because one minute later Lawson scored our first try of the match.

It could not have been simpler. Strokosch won a lineout, Califano peeled around and a gap as wide as the Severn bridge appeared for Lawson to race through and run forty-odd metres for the try. Paterson converted and the score stood at Ospreys 22 – 10 Gloucester Rugby.

With sixty two minutes gone Collazo replaced Califano and three minutes later Narraway came on for Qera. Narraway scarcely had time to get wet before he was yellow-carded three minutes later for using bad language, although it was not directed at a match official. *Sospan fach* Luke!

Hook landed the resultant penalty kick and it was Ospreys 25 – 10 Gloucester Rugby.

Nine minutes from time Azam landed the treble for Gloucester when he became our third player to get himself yellow-carded. This time Marty Holah came over the top at a ruck and Oli helped him back onside. What's wrong with that?

Over the next seven minutes Ospreys made eight substitutions and after one minute of injury time replacement Hibbard, their replacement hooker crossed for another

Ospreys try when he was driven over from a lineout. Hook added the conversion and the scoreline looked pretty bleak at Ospreys 32 – 10 Gloucester Rugby.

We did manage to save some face however, when Lamby ran onto Tindall's kick ahead and touched down to make it Ospreys 32 – 15 Gloucester Rugby. We could not add the conversion and that is how the match ended.

Gloucester were beaten by a display of power and control that we were unable to match on the day but we still scored a couple of nice tries and were badly treated by a lot of refereeing decisions.

Said Dean Ryan: "There were certain things that happened that will make us pretty angry this week... but in terms of the group, nothing has really changed. We have one game to go to reach the knockout stages and I think any team would settle for that scenario at this stage."

Too true Deano.

OSPREYS	GLOUCESTER RUGBY
Try: Hibbard, Williams	**Try:** Lamb, Lawson
Conversion: Hook (2)	**Conversion:** Paterson
Penalty Goal: Hook (6)	**Penalty Goal:** Lamb

OTHER POOL 2 RESULT
Ulster 25 - 24 Bourgoin

Position	Club	Played	Points
1	Gloucester Rugby	5	19
2	Ospreys	5	17
3	Bourgoin	5	7
4	Ulster	5	5

Heineken Cup Pool Two
Kingsholm
Gloucester Rugby 29 – 21 Ulster
kick off 1.00pm Sunday 20 January 2008
Attendance 12,480 : R Poite (France) referee

GLOUCESTER RUGBY

15. I Balshaw 14. J Simpson-Daniel 13. M Tindall 12. A Allen 11. L Vainikolo 10. C Paterson 9. R Lawson 1. N Wood 2. O Azam 3. C Nieto 4. P Buxton 5. M Bortolami 6. A Strokosch 7. A Qera 8. G Delve

Replacements

16. A Titterrell 17. C Califano 18. W James 19. L Narraway 20. G Cooper 21. R Lamb 22. W Walker

ULSTER

15. M Bartholomeusz 14. T Bowe 13. A Trimble 12. P Steinmetz 11. M McCrea 10. Wallace 9. I Boss 1. B Young 2. R Best 3. D Fitzpatrick 4. J Harrison 5. R Caldwell 6. M McCullough 7. N Best 8. G Webb

Replacements

16. N Brady 17. T Court 18. C del Fava 19. N McMillan 20. K Campbell 21. N O'Connor 22. S Mallon

We scored five tries and made it into the knockout stages of the Heineken Cup and yet still the Gloucester team was accused of putting in a patchy performance. There is no pleasing some folk. Perhaps they are confusing Gloucester's performance with the fact that Ulster were a far finer team of rugby players than the team we met earlier in the competition at Ravenhill where they compounded mistake with mistake to put themselves out of contention by half time.

At Kingsholm they gave a far more polished performance and even conspired to put the frighteners on occasionally and score three tries of their own.

We opened our account after nineteen minutes with a Qera try which Chris Paterson promptly converted to make the score Gloucester Rugby 7 – 0 Ulster. With Gloucester in possession Mike Tindall rolled out of a tackle and took off at speed. He was hauled down but succeeded in getting in a pass to Qera who scored.

Two minutes later Ulster responded with a very soft try – the sort you often live to regret. Isaac Boss found a gap and galloped through our defensive line. He fired out a long pass to Bowe who completed the move by crossing in the corner. Wallace converted and the score stood all-square at Gloucester Rugby 7 – 7 Ulster.

Leading up to the break we dominated a series of scrums close to the opposition line and with thirty four minutes gone Lawson found Paterson who set up a ruck. When the ball came back Oli Azam drove forwards and Strokosch took the ball over the Ulster line for our second try. Paterson converted and the score stood at Gloucester Rugby 14 – 7 Ulster.

Four minutes before the break McCrea was yellow carded and the half ended with Gloucester playing against fourteen men but we were unable to take advantage of our numerical superiority.

Half time score Gloucester Rugby 14 – 7 Ulster

Four minutes into the second half we allowed Ulster to score when they were a man down which got the Gloucester support slightly hot under the collar. It happened from a long Balshaw kick. Bowe fielded it and turned the defence with a chip-and-chase. He fielded his own kick and combined with Harrison and Neil Best to keep the move alive. It was Trimble who finally crossed our line to touch down and Wallace converted to put the score level once more at Gloucester Rugby 14 – 14 Ulster.

At this point in the game we struggled slightly to get on terms with our opponents. Particularly their ability to play from deep positions and with fifty one minutes gone Paterson was substituted by Ryan Lamb in the hope that more invention and creativity might result from the change.

With eighteen minutes left we finally found a way through. Simpson-Daniel and Anthony Allen took it close, Azam took it closer still and it was left to Ulster's Bowe to make an inspired tackle on Vainikolo but it could not prevent Qera getting possession and crossing in the corner for his second try of the afternoon. At Gloucester Rugby 19 – 14 Ulster Lamby missed the conversion and on the hour mark Will James came on for Bortolami and four minutes later Titterrell replaced Azam.

With seventy one minutes gone Lamby, up flat where he is at his most devastating threw out a massive pass which cleared both his centres and went straight to the hands of Simpson-Daniel who worked his magic before giving it to Vainikolo who shipped it on to Balsh who touched down for our fourth try and the bonus point, stretching our lead to Gloucester Rugby 24 – 14 Ulster. Again we failed in our conversion attempt but we were still ten points clear with less than ten minutes to go.

Narraway replaced Delve and four minutes later Cooper replaced Lawson and shortly after Walker came on for Tindall.

Three minutes from the finish Ulster put the wind up Gloucester when Bowe scored his second try of the day after O'Connor put a cross kick straight into the waiting hands of McCrea who then gave the inside pass to Bowe to touch down.

O'Connor added the conversion and cut our lead to a trifling three points

which set Gloucester nerves on edge at Gloucester Rugby 24 – 21 Ulster but right on the end of normal time we scored our fifth and final try through Luke Narraway. Again it was generated from Lamb's flat, accurate pass and Narraway took it on the burst to beat the remnants of the Ulster defence to their line.

Once more Lamby's conversion attempt went adrift and just for good measure Qera got himself yellow-carded two minutes into injury time but we were through to the knockout stages of the European Cup.

GLOUCESTER RUGBY	ULSTER
Try: Balshaw, Narraway, Qera, Strokosch	**Try:** Bowe, Trimble
Conversion: Paterson (2)	**Conversion:** O'Connor, Wallace (2)

OTHER POOL 2 RESULT
Bourgoin 21 - 28 Ospreys

Position	Club	Played	Points
1	Gloucester Rugby	6	24
2	Ospreys	6	21
3	Bourgoin	6	8
4	Ulster	6	5

Gloucester Rugby 18 – 17 London Wasps

kick off 3.00pm Saturday 26 January 2008
Attendance 16,200 : D Pearson referee

GLOUCESTER RUGBY

15. W Walker 14. I Balshaw 13. J Simpson-Daniel 12. M Tindall 11. J Bailey 10. R Lamb 9. R Lawson 1. N Wood 2. O Azam 3. C Nieto 4. P Buxton 5. W James 6. L Narraway 7. Hazell 8. G Delve

Replacements

16. J Paul 17. P Collazo 18. D Tuohy 9. A Strokosch 20. G Cooper 21. A Allen 22. M Foster

LONDON WASPS

15. J Lewsey 14. B Hoadley 13. F Waters 12. D Waldouck 11. D Doherty 10. D Cipriani 9. M McMillan 1. T Payne 2. J Ward 3. P Vickery 4. T Palmer 5. G Skivington 6. J Haskell 7. T Rees 8. L Dallaglio

Replacements

16. J Buckland 17. N Adams 18. R Birkett 19. J Hart 20. S Amor 21. D Walder 22. D Leo

In a match full of nervous energy and vitriol Phil Vickery got the full treatment, having to deal with at least two but mostly three Gloucester tacklers every time he found himself in possession. The Gloucester players were adamant afterwards that they did not single out their ex-captain for special treatment but it certainly looked that way to the untrained eye...

We went into the lead at Gloucester Rugby 3 – 0 London Wasps after four minutes following a Ryan Lamb penalty when a scrum fell apart after Wasps could not deal with the ferocious Gloucester scrummage. Narraway went off with a blood injury after twelve minutes to be replaced by Strokosch and four minutes later Lamb struck another penalty to put us six points clear at Gloucester Rugby 6 – 0 London Wasps

148

when their scrum half Mark McMillan was judged to be offside. All in all a nice steady opening to a match but we let it slip from the restart when James fumbled his take and Narraway encroached offside.

Cipriani landed the points and Wasps only points of the half to move the scoreline on to Gloucester Rugby 6 – 3 London Wasps.

One minute later Dallaglio was unable to control himself and dived on the

ball in a ruck which resulted in another three points when Lamb landed the resultant penalty kick.

With twenty three minutes on the clock Narraway returned to the pitch and at Gloucester Rugby 9 – 3 London Wasps the visitors were on the back foot. We forced them to defend for long periods on end and they predictably resorted to what Wasps do best...

Consequently on the half hour mark they were reduced to fourteen men when blindside flanker James Haskell was yellow-carded for preventing Narraway from releasing the ball.

Although we cranked up the tempo a notch, we were unable to make our advantage of the extra man tell and Haskell returned to the pitch. As he did so Balshaw was held just short of the line and this time Palmer killed the ball and got himself a siesta in the sin bin while Lamby knocked over the penalty kick to put us comfortably in the lead at Gloucester Rugby 12 – 3 London Wasps.

Half time score Gloucester Rugby 12 – 3 London Wasps

Three minutes into the second half Lamb knocked over another penalty from a long way out. It put us firmly in the driving seat at Gloucester Rugby 15 – 3 London Wasps.

One minute later Foster replaced Bailey and one minute after that Lamb added another penalty to his tally to put us fifteen points clear at Gloucester Rugby 18 – 3 London Wasps.

On the hour mark Jeremy Paul came on for Azam and Bailey came back onto the pitch after treatment and we were going along quite happily until Ryan Lamb was sent to the bin. Collazo was brought on as a replacement for Nick Wood who went off for treatment and Wasps succeeded in taking advantage of our reduced number to score a try when they kicked the penalty to the corner. Instead of the expected catch-and-drive the ball went straight back to their replacement hooker James Buckland and he scooted down the five-metre channel to score the first try of the day.

Cipriani added the conversion and at Gloucester Rugby 18 – 10 London Wasps, and with our side reduced to fourteen men, things were starting to get a little nervy in the Gloucester ranks.

The amber alert was upped to a red alert when Wasps scored another try in the sixty fifth minute putting them three points behind at Gloucester Rugby 18 – 15 London Wasps. It developed from a mis-kick from Cipriani which caught Willie Walker off his guard. Bailey backed him up but Wasps turned over possession and Vickery made some ground before getting it to Haskell who fed the scoring pass to Waldouck who touched down.

When Cipriani converted to put his side a single point behind us loud and long were the celebrations of the Wasps supporters in the stands.

We substituted Strokosch for Delve and Allen for Tindall on sixty six minutes and prepared to repel the inevitable Wasps onslaught.

On seventy one minutes Nick Wood returned to take his place in the Gloucester pack which had taken over the running of the game. They expertly shut down the game with straight, short forward breaks, kept possession and prevented Wasps from getting their chance.

It worked. We came away with four league points and a renewed sense of confidence that we could pull off victories in close matches against the street-wise teams in the Premiership.

To put the icing on the cake Bristol and Bath lost their away matches to Worcester and Saracens respectively.

<table>
<tr><td>**GLOUCESTER RUGBY**
Penalty Goal: Lamb (6)</td><td>**LONDON WASPS**
Try: Buckland, Waldouck
Conversion: Cipriani (2)
Penalty Goal: Cipriani</td></tr>
</table>

OTHER RESULTS
Sale Sharks 20 – 13 Harlequins
Leicester Tigers 41 - 14 Newcastle Falcons
Worcester Warriors 25 - 5 Bristol Rugby
Saracens 26 - 20 Bath Rugby
Leeds Carnegie 24 - 26 London Irish

CLUB	P	W	D	L	F	A	TF	TA	TB	LB	P
Gloucester Rugby	11	9	0	2	284	171	32	20	3	2	41

Bath Rugby	11	8	0	3	287	192	29	15	3	2	37
Leicester Tigers	11	8	0	3	255	189	31	17	3	1	36
Saracens	11	7	0	4	267	233	27	24	1	3	32
Sale Sharks	11	7	0	4	233	203	22	22	3	1	32
Harlequins	11	5	0	6	227	252	25	30	3	4	27
London Irish	11	5	0	6	212	210	21	21	1	3	24
London Wasps	11	4	2	5	238	209	25	19	1	3	24
Newcastle Falcons	11	5	0	6	185	245	19	28	1	2	23
Bristol Rugby	11	4	1	6	172	216	18	21	1	1	19
Worcester Warriors	11	1	1	9	178	244	20	26	0	5	11
Leeds Carnegie	11	1	0	10	181	355	19	45	0	2	6

Gloucester Rugby 13 – 20 Leicester Tigers

Kick off Saturday 9 February 2008
Attendance 12,597 : A Spreadbury referee

GLOUCESTER RUGBY

15. J Bailey 14. J Simpson-Daniel 13. J Adams 12. A Allen 11. M Foster 10. W Walker 9. R Lawson 1. N Wood 2. O Azam 3. J Forster 4. P Buxton 5. W James 6. A Strokosch 7. A Hazell 8. A Balding

Replacements

16. J Paul 17. A Dickinson 18. J Pendlebury 19. A Titterrell 20. G Cooper 21. A James 22. C Sharples

LEICESTER TIGERS

15. J Murphy 14. T Varndell 13. A Erinle 12. A Mauger 11. O Smith   10. A Goode 9. C Laussucq 1. M Ayerza 2. G Chuter 3. A Moreno 4. T Croft 5. M Wentzel 6. M Corry 7. B Herring 8. J Crane

Replacements

16. B Kayser 17. D Young 18. G Gillanders 19. B Deacon 20. F Murphy 21. I Humphreys 22. S Vesty

This was Round Seventeen brought forward because of the involvement of Leicester Tigers, London Wasps and Saracens in the EDF Energy Cup semi-finals. The other semi-final matches which were moved were: Saracens versus Worcester Warriors on 10 February 2008 and London Wasps versus Sale Sharks on 15 April 2008.

The other three matches were played over the weekend Friday 21 to Sunday 23 March 2008.

On the Friday night Leeds Carnegie beat Newcastle at Headingley Carnegie (where Leeds' Chris Blackett set a new record for the fastest Premiership try when he scored with 8.28 seconds on the clock); on the Saturday, Bath Rugby beat London Irish at The Rec and went top of the league with a game in hand over Gloucester and Leicester; on the Sunday

NEC Harlequins beat Bristol Rugby at the Memorial Ground 15 – 28, claiming a maximum points win and putting themselves fourth in the Premiership table.

Back to Kingsholm: There was no score for thirty four minutes when Goode got the pass from a lineout and fed Varndell who came in off his wing at pace. With the extra man in their line the ball was worked to Smith who went outside Bailey and crossed our line for the first score of the day. Goode converted from the touchline and the visitors went into a clear lead at Gloucester Rugby 0 – 7 Leicester Tigers.

Three minutes later Will James was yellow-carded along with Leicester's openside Herring and it was a full forty minutes before Gloucester could find a way onto the scoreboard which was achieved through a Willie Walker penalty.

Half time score Gloucester Rugby 3 – 7 Leicester Tigers

With eight minutes of the second half gone Leicester infringed at a lineout but instead of going for the posts Walker opted to kick for the corner. The expected catch-and-drive did not materialise however. Oli Azam put in a short one to Bucko jumping at number two who tossed it straight back to him off the top and Oli clattered over for a nicely-worked try straight out of the London Wasps handbook as demonstrated the week before.

Walker added the conversion from the touchline and we went ahead at Gloucester Rugby 10 – 7 Leicester Tigers.

With a quarter of an hour of the second half gone Goode slammed over another penalty when we were caught offside, drawing the scores level at Gloucester Rugby 10 – 10 Leicester Tigers.

We replaced Lawson with Cooper and Paul came on for Azam and then with sixty two minutes gone Walker slotted another penalty for us putting us back in front at Gloucester Rugby 13 – 10 Leicester.

It was a short lived lead, however. Three minutes later Goode kicked another penalty to draw level again, at Gloucester Rugby 13 – 13 Leicester Tigers when we were penalised for hands-in at a ruck.

Fifteen minutes to go and all level on the scoreboard, when you are playing Leicester, is a hard one to call.

With sixty six minutes on the clock we replaced Balding with Pendlebury and one minute later Gloucester supporters' blood froze when Leicester utilised a speciality of theirs and attacked from a set piece.

153

They controlled a scrum just inside their own half and then Goode made a half-break and got the ball out to Mauger whose angle of run took him through our first line of defence. We regrouped quickly but Erinle was coming in from the Shedside wing and aiming for the clubhouse corner. His line took him outside and away from Jack Foster and Andy Hazell. Give Leicester their due, it was a breathtaking piece of football.

Goode converted and with thirteen minutes to go we were seven points behind at Gloucester Rugby 13 – 20 Leicester Tigers.

We launched a number of attacks through both forwards and backs and forced them back in the set pieces and with one minute of normal time left Herring infringed by preventing Cooper from taking a quick penalty and he was red-carded as it was his second yellow card that day but the damage had been done. Leicester regrouped and although Simpson-Daniel came screaming through Murphy got back to make the tackle and following that a pass to Foster which might have resulted in a try went astray.

It was a close-run thing but it is a cold, hard fact of life that close-run does not get you any league points.

GLOUCESTER RUGBY	LEICESTER TIGERS
Try: Azam	**Try:** Erinle, Smith
Conversion: Walker	**Conversion:** Goode (2)
Penalty Goal: Walker (2)	**Penalty Goal:** Goode (2)

OTHER ROUND 17 RESULT
Saracens 19 - 6 Worcester

CLUB	P	W	D	L	F	A	TF	TA	TB	LB	P
Gloucester Rugby	12	9	0	3	297	191	33	22	3	3	42
Leicester Tigers	12	9	0	3	307	205	31	16	3	2	41
Bath Rugby	11	8	0	3	255	189	31	17	3	1	36
Saracens	12	8	0	4	286	239	28	24	1	3	36
Sale Sharks	11	7	0	4	233	203	22	22	3	1	32
Harlequins	11	5	0	6	227	252	25	30	3	4	27
London Irish	11	5	0	6	212	210	21	21	1	3	24
London Wasps	11	4	2	5	238	209	25	19	1	3	24
Newcastle Falcons	11	5	0	6	185	245	19	28	1	2	23
Bristol Rugby	11	4	1	6	172	216	18	21	1	1	19
Worcester Warriors	12	1	1	10	184	263	20	27	0	5	11
Leeds Carnegie	11	1	0	10	181	355	19	45	0	2	6

Bristol Rugby 29 – 26 Gloucester Rugby

Kickoff 3.00pm Sunday 17 February 2008
Attendance 11,418 : W Barnes referee

BRISTOL RUGBY

15. L Arscott 14. L Robinson 13. R Higgitt 12. D Hill 11. D Lemi 10. J Strange 9. B O'Riordan 1. D Crompton 2. S Linklater 3. J Hobson 4. R Winters 5. S Hohneck 6. M Salter 7. J El Abd 8. A Blowers

Replacements

16. M Regan 17. A Clarke 18. G Llewellyn 19. A T Vaeluaga 20. G Beveridge 21. S Cox 22. J Taumalolo

GLOUCESTER RUGBY

15. I Balshaw 14. J Simpson-Daniel 13. J Adams 12. A Allen 11. L Vainikolo 10. C Paterson 9. G Cooper 1. N Wood 2. J Paul 3. C Nieto 4. W James 5. M Bortolami 6. L Narraway 7. A Hazell 8. G Delve

Replacements

16. A Titterrell 17. A Dickinson 18. P Buxton 19. A Strokosch 20. R Lawson 21. W Walker 22. M Foster

Bristol went six points to nil ahead in the first eight minutes courtesy of standoff half Jason Strange with two penalties on four and eight minutes. But then we notched up two tries in as many minutes. The first coming after fourteen minutes through Simpson-Daniel when he finished off a break by Jack Adams. Big Les straightened up the line following a lineout drive and Jack Adams stepped inside. Paul and Paterson combined and sent Sinbad over in the corner.

Two minutes later he returned the favour when he put in a kick-and-chase which Adams touched down. Both of Paterson's conversion attempts went astray and the score stood at Bristol Rugby 6 – 10 Gloucester Rugby after twenty one minutes when Strange knocked over another penalty to

155

bring his team to within a point of us at Bristol Rugby 9 – 10 Gloucester Rugby.

Six minutes later we scored our third try when Anthony Allen intercepted a Jason Strange pass near the halfway line and sped to the Bristol line to touch down. Paterson made no mistake this time with his conversion attempt and the score moved on to a reasonable Bristol Rugby 9 – 17 Gloucester Rugby.

With three tries inside the first half hour, Gloucester looked well-poised for

another bonus point. We were all half-expecting Bristol to fall apart at the seams but nothing prepared us for what was about to unfold.

On thirty three minutes Bristol hooker Scott Linklater scored a try from a catch-and-drive at a Bristol lineout and Strange converted, putting his side only a single point away from us again at Bristol Rugby 16 – 17 Gloucester Rugby.

On thirty six minutes Marco Bortolami was yellow-carded and two minutes later the home side took full advantage of their superior numbers with another catch-and-drive from a five-metre Bristol lineout. This time it was Hobson who was driven over and once more Strange converted to put his side in the lead at the break at Bristol 23 – 17 Gloucester.

Half time score Bristol Rugby 23 – 17 Gloucester Rugby

Having leaked fourteen points in a matter of six minutes it is fairly easy to guess the gist of Dean Ryan's half-time speech to his troops but there was no improvement in their play in the second half.

Strange kicked another penalty on the forty five minute mark putting his side further ahead at Bristol Rugby 26 – 17 Gloucester Rugby and on forty seven minutes Paterson pulled the three points back with a Gloucester conversion and the score stood at Bristol Rugby 26 – 20 Gloucester Rugby.

We made a number of substitutions bringing on Titterrell for Jeremy Paul and Strokosch for Narraway at forty seven minutes; Lawson for Cooper on forty eight minutes and Walker for Paterson on the fifty four minute mark but they pinned us down in our own territory for most of the second half and on sixty four minutes Strange dropped a goal to put us even further behind at Bristol 29 – 20 Gloucester.

Buxton replaced Will James on sixty five minutes and four minutes later Walker added a penalty to our tally putting the score at Bristol Rugby 29 – 23 Gloucester Rugby.

With seventy one minutes gone he kicked another penalty for us and at Bristol Rugby 29 – 26 Gloucester Rugby, it was the last score of the match.
When you win a derby match you get the bragging rights. Bristol were loud in their delight and we slunk off home in silence with our tails between our legs.

BRISTOL RUGBY
Try: Hobson, Linklater
Conversion: Strange (2)
Penalty Goal: Strange (4)

GLOUCESTER RUGBY
Try: Adams, Allen, S-Daniel
Conversion: Paterson
Penalty Goal: Paterson, Walker (2)

OTHER RESULTS
Sale Sharks 29 - 3 Leeds Carnegie
Bath Rugby 34 - 42 London Wasps
Harlequins 36 - 15 Worcester Warriors
London Irish 22 – 13 Leicester Tigers
Falcons 16 - 14 Saracens

CLUB	P	W	D	L	F	A	TF	TA	TB	LB	P
Gloucester Rugby	13	9	0	4	323	220	36	24	3	4	43
Leicester Tigers	13	9	0	4	320	227	32	17	3	2	41
Bath Rugby	12	8	0	4	289	231	35	22	4	1	37
Saracens	13	8	0	5	300	255	29	25	1	4	37
Sale Sharks	12	8	0	4	262	206	24	22	3	1	36
Harlequins	12	6	0	6	263	267	30	32	4	4	32
London Wasps	12	5	2	5	280	243	30	23	2	3	29
London Irish	12	6	0	6	234	223	22	22	1	3	28
Newcastle Falcons	12	6	0	6	201	259	20	29	1	2	27
Bristol Rugby	12	5	1	6	201	242	20	24	1	1	23
Worcester Warriors	13	1	1	11	199	299	22	32	0	5	11
Leeds Carnegie	12	1	0	11	184	384	19	47	0	2	6

Gloucester Rugby 28 – 20 Newcastle Falcons

Kick off 3.00pm Saturday 23 February 2008
Attendance 13,047 : M Fox referee

GLOUCESTER RUGBY
15. W Walker 14. J Simpson-Daniel 13. J Adams 12. A Allen
11. M Foster 10. R Lamb 9. G Cooper 1. N Wood 2. A Titterrell
3. J Forster 4. W James 5. A Brown 6. P Buxton 7. A Hazell 8.
L Narraway

Replacements
16. O Azam 17. C Califano 18. J Pendlebury 19. A Qera 20. M
Prendergast 21. A James 22. J Bailey

NEWCASTLE FALCONS
15. T May 14. O Phillips 13. T Dillon 12. A Tait 11. J Rudd 10.
S Jones   9. L Dickson 1. J McDonnell 2. M Thompson 3. C
Hayman 4. A Perry   5. M Sorenson 6. G Parling 7. B Woods
8. P Dowson

Replacements
16. A Long 17. D Wilson 18. T Swinson 19. B Wilson 20. J
Grindal   21. J Shaw 22. T Visser

Newcastle started at full speed ahead, determined to rattle
Gloucester and take advantage of any lingering doubts from
the previous week's damaging loss at Bristol.
Despite this we landed two early penalties, courtesy of Willie
Walker at eleven minutes and twenty three minutes and we
were six points to nil ahead. Our first came when Jack Adams
fielded a wayward pass from a scrum by Gareth Cooper. He
raced thirty metres upfield before offloading to Walker who
was brought down. When the visitors were penalised for killing
the ball at the breakdown, Walker slammed over his first of the
day. The second came when Newcastle infringed following a
series of powerful Gloucester forward drives.
Three minutes after our second penalty their standoff Steve
Jones got himself yellow-carded when he deliberately knocked

forward while intercepting a Gloucester pass and we looked a shoo-in for more points in his absence.

It took seven minutes to force a mistake from the visitors and Walker

converted the penalty award into three more points and at Gloucester Rugby 9 – 0 Newcastle Falcons, and temporarily facing fourteen players we were looking very comfortable indeed, thank you.

But sport - particularly rugby - is not a precise science; otherwise it would be performed in a test tube or on a computer screen. Gareth Cooper was turned over deep in the Newcastle half and winger Ollie Phillips belted it way, way downfield. It was much too far to technically qualify as a chip-and-chase but he followed it up, beating Lamb in the footrace.

Walker got to the ball but somehow Phillips collared him and succeeded in wresting possession from him, running on to touch down under the posts. Fullback Tom May added the easy conversion and suddenly they were only two points adrift at Gloucester Rugby 9 – 7 Newcastle Falcons.

Then, one minute before the break, they added a second try - and five more points to our woes - when somehow Tom May found a way through our defence when Carl Hayman gave him the ball in our twenty two. He made his way behind our posts once more added the easy conversion to put us behind, bemused and beside ourselves at Gloucester Rugby 9 – 14 Newcastle Falcons.

Half time score Gloucester Rugby 9 – 14 Newcastle Falcons

Five minutes into the half Bailey was substituted for Jack Adams and at six minutes May knocked over his third kick of the day with a penalty which nudged his team further ahead at Gloucester Rugby 9 – 17 Newcastle Falcons.

At forty eight minutes Jack Adams returned to the fray but things were not going quite as well as we had hoped for and our miseries were compounded when scrum half Lee Dixon took a quick penalty and got the ball into the strike zone. It was May who dropped the inevitable goal and with an eleven points deficit at Gloucester Rugby 9 – 20 Newcastle Falcons, the team and supporters alike were reeling like a dazed boxer clinging onto his opponent for dear life at the prospect of a third defeat on the trot.

At fifty seven minutes Azam replaced Titterrell and on the hour mark Qera came on for Will James.

At sixty two minutes Mark Foster put up a garryowen and brilliantly claimed possession of it. Cooper and Lamb worked together and when Lamby sent out a long ball Jack Adams straightened the line, giving Simpson-Daniel the space he needed to weave his magic and touch down to put us back in contention at Gloucester Rugby 14 – 20 Newcastle Falcons. Walker converted and it was "game on" at Gloucester Rugby 16 – 20 Newcastle Falcons as the home side's confidence was rekindled.

Gloucester threw attack after attack at the Newcastle line by way of our forwards, notably Azam, Bucko, Hazey and Nick Wood (in alphabetical
order). Newcastle defended desperately but it was clear that it was only a
matter of time before we found a way through.

On seventy minutes Bailey came on for Lamb and three minutes later a marauding Willie Walker broke through the first line of defence with an elegant sidestep. The ball came back to Sinbad who made a run down the right with Gloucester players streaming up everywhere in support like extras in *Zulu*. It was down to Hazell to take it down the left and when Bailey hove into view he sent him over in the corner with a beautifully weighted pass.

At Gloucester Rugby 21 – 20 Newcastle Falcons we held the slimmest of leads and Walker's missed conversion attempt did nothing to ease our nerviness.

There were seven minutes left to play and decisions had to be made: Did we defend a one point lead? Did we seek to improve it and risk a penalty goal or a runaway try against us?

We elected to play the clock down using our time-honoured tactic of a series of short, determined forward drives. Then, with a minute to go, they turned us over in our own backyard. They moved it to the left and May set himself for a drop goal attempt.

Narraway read the situation perfectly – as did the rest of the team and thirteen-odd thousand Gloucester supporters. Have you noticed how situations like this tend to take on a slow-motion dreamlike quality as if they were part of a feature film? Narraway moved up to the kick far too slowly for our liking but - wonder of wonders - he managed to charge it down and thirteen thousand voices screamed with the release of tension. We knew the game was won then but it was still not over.

The hero of the moment deftly gathered and ran. Qera appeared on his shoulder calling for it and Narraway shipped it on. Qera touched it down with eighty minutes on the clock. Walker denied our visitors the losing bonus point when he converted and the game was over at Gloucester Rugby 28 – 20 Newcastle Falcons.

It had been a struggle, particularly at the lineout, where we were rocky on occasions; and at times we failed to cope effectively when the ball was on the ground, an area where the visitors excelled, giving them a great platform from which to perform.

But we won. It might not have been pretty at times but it is better to win ugly than to not win at all, as the saying goes and we were still top of the league.

GLOUCESTER RUGBY
Try: Bailey, Qera, S-Daniel
Conversion: Walker (2)
Penalty Goal: Walker (3)

NEWCASTLE FALCONS
Try: May, Phillips
Conversion: May (2)
Penalty Goal: May

OTHER RESULTS
Worcester Warriors 11 - 12 London Irish
Leicester Tigers 11 - 14 Sale Sharks
London Wasps 32 - 30 Bristol Rugby
Leeds Carnegie15 - 34 Bath Rugby
Saracens 6 - 15 Harlequins

CLUB	P	W	D	L	F	A	TF	TA	TB	LB	P
Gloucester Rugby	14	10	0	4	351	240	39	26	3	4	47
Leicester Tigers	14	9	0	5	331	241	33	18	3	3	42
Bath Rugby	13	9	0	4	323	246	39	24	5	1	42
Sale Sharks	13	9	0	4	276	217	25	23	3	1	40
Saracens	14	8	0	6	306	270	29	27	1	4	37
Harlequins	13	7	0	6	278	273	32	32	4	4	36
London Wasps	13	6	2	5	312	273	34	27	3	3	34
London Irish	13	7	0	6	246	234	22	23	1	3	32
Newcastle Falcons	13	6	0	7	221	287	22	32	1	2	27
Bristol Rugby	13	5	1	7	231	274	24	28	2	2	25
Worcester Warriors	14	1	1	12	210	311	23	32	0	6	12
Leeds Carnegie	13	1	0	12	199	418	21	51	0	2	6

HARLEQUINS 30 – 25 GLOUCESTER RUGBY

Kick off 2.45pm Saturday 1 March 2008
Attendance 12,638 : S Davey referee

HARLEQUINS

15. M Brown 14. T Williams 13. H Luscombe 12. T Masson 11. U Monye 10. A Jarvis 9. D Care 1. C Jones 2. T Fuga 3. M Ross 4. J Percival   5. N Spanghero 6. C Robshaw 7. W Skinner 8. N Easter

Replacements

16. C Brooker 17. J Brooks 18. G Robson 19. C Hala'ufia 20. A Gomarsall 21. C Malone 22. de W Barry

GLOUCESTER RUGBY

15. I Balshaw 14. J Simpson-Daniel 13. J Adams 12. A Allen 11. L Vainikolo 10. W Walker 9. R Lawson 1. N Wood 2. O Azam 3. C Nieto 4. P Buxton 5. A Brown 6. A Strokosch 7. A Qera 8. L Narraway

Replacements

16. A Titterrell 17. A Dickinson 18. M Bortolami 19. G Delve 20. G Cooper 21. C Paterson 22. M Foster

The home side's record against Gloucester is a horror story for them. From their last eleven meetings since 6 February 2001 having beaten us only once - on 5 February 2005 – but this match degenerated into a horror story for Gloucester.

The scoring started with a penalty to Harlequins on fifteen minutes, easily slotted by Jarvis, and two minutes later we replied with a try from Jack Adams. Walker charged down a kick by Jarvis near our twenty two and Adams pounced on the loose ball, running over seventy metres to touch down under the posts. Walker's conversion attempt was wonky, an unfortunate trademark of his game all afternoon, a fact which would subsequently cost us dear.

On nineteen minutes Monye somehow got possession unchallenged from the restart and took it perilously close before he was dragged down. Harlequins recovered possession and loosehead Ceri Jones was driven over, putting the score at Harlequins 8 – 5 Gloucester Rugby. Jarvis converted and the score was Harlequins 10 – 5 Gloucester Rugby.

The points seemed to be coming thick and fast from both teams and on

twenty two minutes Vainikolo fielded Brown's kick and put in a threatening run down the left wing. Buxton moved in and his scoring pass to Balshaw put us level at Harlequins 10 – 10 Gloucester Rugby. Walker succeeded with this conversion and we went two points ahead at NEC Harlequins 10 – 12 Gloucester Rugby.

Walker stretched our lead by another three points to Harlequins 10 – 15 Gloucester Rugby with a penalty after thirty one minutes and on thirty six minutes we scored our second try, this time through Anthony Allen. Sinbad stepped in off his wing and put the Harlequins defence into disarray before passing to Allen who scorched in to make the score Harlequins 10 – 20 Gloucester Rugby. Willie Walker's conversion attempt failed and Harlequins scored on the forty minute mark when a Gloucester clearance kick failed to find touch. Care passed to Jarvis, the ball came back from a ruck and Brown found his way through a defensive gap to put his side back in contention at Harlequins 15 – 20 Gloucester Rugby.

Jarvis converted and they were only three points adrift at half time.

Half time score Harlequins 17 – 20 Gloucester Rugby

One minute into the second half Mark Foster replaced Jack Adams and ten minutes later Andy Titterrell came on for Oli Azam. Then on fifty four minutes Harlequins drew level at Harlequins 20 – 20 Gloucester Rugby through a Jarvis penalty kick when we were penalised for offside and a minute later Gareth Delve replaced Luke Narraway.

It was an extremely hard game to call, with Gloucester's set pieces suddenly deteriorating beyond all recognition and yet we still managed to score a try for the bonus point on fifty seven minutes when Simpson-Daniel scorched through a gap to score. At Harlequins 20 – 25 Gloucester Rugby Walker missed the conversion and the game still hung in the balance.

On sixty two minutes Bortolami replaced Qera and five minutes later Dickinson came on for Wood. Then in the sixty ninth minute Foster put in a high tackle and Jarvis scored the penalty to put his side only two points adrift at Harlequins 23 – 25 Gloucester Rugby.

On seventy one minutes Harlequins strung together a number of drives and Malone, who had come on as a replacement only one minute before, got the ball to Robson who was also a replacement player.

Robson somehow managed to beat Sinbad on the outside and crossed our line to score wide on the left.

They added the conversion and Gloucester never got the opportunity to launch another attack. The game finished at Harlequins 30 – 25 Gloucester Rugby.

Ours had been a frustrating performance. Self-inflicted cracks had appeared in our armour and a number of Premiership and European clubs would be rubbing their hands at the prospect of adding to our discomforts.

HARLEQUINS
Try: Brown, Fuga, Robson
Conversion: Jarvis (2), Malone
Penalty Goal: Jarvis (3)

GLOUCESTER RUGBY
Try: Adams, Allen, Balshaw, S-Daniel
Conversion: Walker
Penalty Goal: Walker

OTHER RESULTS
Sale Sharks 15 - 22 Worcester Warriors
London Irish 27 - 24 Saracens
Leicester Tigers 34 - 21 Leeds Carnegie
Bristol Rugby 9 - 19 Bath Rugby

CLUB	P	W	D	L	F	A	TF	TA	TB	LB	P
Gloucester Rugby	15	10	0	5	376	270	43	29	4	5	49
Leicester Tigers	15	10	0	5	365	262	38	20	4	3	47
Bath Rugby	14	10	0	4	342	255	40	24	5	1	46
Sale Sharks	14	9	0	5	291	239	25	24	3	2	41
Harlequins	14	8	0	6	308	298	35	36	4	4	40
Saracens	15	8	0	7	330	297	31	29	1	5	38
London Irish	14	8	0	6	273	258	24	25	1	3	36
London Wasps	13	6	2	5	312	273	34	27	3	3	34
Newcastle Falcons	13	6	0	7	221	287	22	32	1	2	27
Bristol Rugby	14	5	1	8	240	293	24	29	2	2	25
Worcester Warriors	15	2	1	12	232	326	24	32	0	0	16
Leeds Carnegie	14	1	0	13	220	452	23	56	0	0	6

Gloucester Rugby 34 – 14 London Irish

Kick off 5.30pm Saturday 8 March 2008
Attendance 12,354 : D Rose referee

GLOUCESTER RUGBY
15. J Bailey 14. J Simpson-Daniel 13. J Adams 12. A Allen 11.
M Foster 10. W Walker 9. G Cooper 1. N Wood 2. A Titterrell
3. J Forster 4. D Tuohy 5. W James 6. P Buxton 7. A Hazell 8.
A Qera

Replacements
16. O Azam 17. C Califano 18. J Pendlebury 19. J Paul 20. M
Prendergast 21. C Sharples 22. D Norton

LONDON IRISH
15. P Hewat 14. T Ojo 13. G Tiesi 12. S Mapusua 11. S
Tagicakibau 10. M Catt 9. W Fury 1. D Murphy 2. D Paice 3. F
Rautenbach 4. K Roche 5. B Casey 6. J Manuel Leguizamon
7. S Armitage 8. R Thorpe

Replacements
16. C Dermody 17. S Macki 18. T Lea'aetoa 19. G Johnson
20. D Danaher 21. R Blake 22. E Hickey

With most of our senior players on international duty or injured
we called on a very inexperienced squad to face the Irish.
They came down the M4 brimming with confidence and from
the very first whistle sought to intimidate in word and deed with
as cynical a display of rugby as you are ever likely to see.
More credit to the Gloucester team then, who put in a
remarkable performance in driving rain, excelling in areas
where you would have expected them to struggle, like the
lineout and the drive from the ruck, to seal a richly-deserved
victory of exuberant youth over cynical experience.
We opened our account nine minutes into the match with a try
by Nick Wood. Will James won the lineout and the drive
angled infield. Bucko carried forward off the fringe and when
the ball came back Walker chipped it through. Mapusua could

not hold the ball but Nick Wood could and he slammed over for the try. Walker converted and we were on our way at Gloucester Rugby 7 – 0 London Irish.

On twelve minutes we scored our second try. This time through Jack Adams after Bailey, at fullback, sent a long kick downfield and Leguizamon made a hash of hacking it forward. Jack Adams however, had better fortune with his hacking and fell on the ball which kindly rebounded off an upright for him. Again Walker converted and at Gloucester Rugby 14 – 0 London Irish, our visitors were showing signs of petulance at their inability to get off the mark.

In the eighteenth minute they finally scored with a Peter Hewat penalty putting the score at Gloucester Rugby 14 – 3 London Irish.

Then with twenty three minutes on the clock we scored our third try when Walker kicked and for the second time that afternoon it rebounded off an Irish player. This time it was Mike Catt.

Qera stopped the ball with his foot and Mark Foster pounced on it to carry over the line and behind the posts to make Walker's conversion a formality and move the score on to Gloucester Rugby 21 – 3 London Irish.

On the half hour mark Titterrell was temporarily replaced by Azam while a blood injury received attention. A decision which was to have consequences for Gloucester when Oli was yellow-carded shortly after.

Titterrell was cut in a boxing match on the ground with an unspecified Irish player and on thirty two minutes Willie Walker knocked over the resultant penalty to put us twenty one points clear at Gloucester Rugby 24 – 3 London Irish. It transpired that Oli responded to Irish skulduggery at a ruck and was yellow-carded while Hewat hit the resultant penalty over the crossbar to double the Irish scoreline at Gloucester Rugby 24 – 6 London Irish.

On thirty nine minutes Qera was replaced by Titterrell when we needed a hooker for the Gloucester scrummage and there were no more scores in the first half.

Half time score Gloucester Rugby 24 – 6 London Irish

With six minutes of the second half gone, Azam returned from the sin bin and was promptly replaced by Qera. Then one minute later Hewat slotted another penalty, putting the score at Gloucester Rugby 24 – 9 London Irish.

166

When we allowed them to capitalise on a Gloucester mistake and score a try in the fiftieth minute, the old nerves started jangling again. We kept possession through a number of phases but Walker tried to force an off-load at the tackle and Ojo was on it in a flash, intercepting the ill-advised pass and racing the intervening sixty five metres to touch down behind our line, putting the score at Gloucester Rugby 24 – 14 London Irish. Then Hewat's conversion attempt failed, leaving the points difference between the two teams unchanged at ten.

On fifty four minutes Charlie Sharples replaced Jack Adams and then, right on the hour mark, Walker stretched our lead by another three points with a penalty kick, putting the score at Gloucester Rugby 27 – 14 London Irish and four minutes later Prendergast replaced Cooper.

With seven minutes of ordinary time left Paice pulled down a Gloucester drive and got a yellow card for his trouble. Walker put it safely in the corner, seeking to take advantage of Gloucester's superior number and Tuohy, who played a blinder all afternoon, set up the drive. It was fitting that Paice's opposite number, Andy Titterrell should finish off the move with a try, although referee Rose did need the video ref's assistance in awarding it. And Walker supplied the extras to put the final score at Gloucester Rugby 34 – 14 London Irish.

With three minutes of time left, Mike Catt was forced to leave the field leaking claret everywhere from a deep cut in his face, to be replaced by Hickey.

Catt's loud and indignant complaints about his injury – caused by Andy Hazell's "swinging arm" - were almost laughable coming from a member of a team which had come to Kingsholm intent on roughing up and intimidating a younger, less-experienced team. For the Gloucester faithful there was a certain amount of satisfaction in seeing him hoist by his own team's petard and we certainly let him know our thoughts on the matter...

The match finished at Gloucester Rugby 34 – 14 London Irish. A fair result because Gloucester were certainly twenty points better than their visitors on the day. With towering performances from Tuohy on his team debut, Will James, Nick Wood and Andy Hazell who combined to create a team performance that bewildered Irish and stopped them in their tracks.

GLOUCESTER RUGBY

Try: Adams, Foster, Titterrell, Wood
Conversion: Walker (4)
Penalty Goal: Walker (2)

LONDON IRISH

Try: Ojo
Penalty Goal: Hewat (3)

OTHER RESULTS

Bath Rugby 22 - 11 Newcastle Falcons
Worcester Warriors 23 - 19 Leicester Tigers
Leeds Carnegie 13 - 30 Bristol Rugby
London Wasps 29 - 25 Harlequins
Saracens 24 - 20 Sale Sharks

CLUB	P	W	D	L	F	A	TF	TA	TB	LB	P
Gloucester Rugby	16	11	0	5	410	284	47	30	5	5	54
Bath Rugby	15	11	0	4	364	266	41	25	5	1	50
Leicester Tigers	16	10	0	6	384	285	39	23	4	4	48
Sale Sharks	15	9	0	6	311	263	27	26	3	3	42
Saracens	16	9	0	7	354	317	33	31	1	5	42
Harlequins	15	8	0	7	333	327	38	38	4	5	41
London Wasps	14	7	2	5	341	298	36	30	3	3	38
London Irish	15	8	0	7	287	292	25	29	1	3	36
Bristol Rugby	15	6	1	8	270	306	28	30	3	2	30
Newcastle Falcons	14	6	0	8	232	309	23	33	1	2	27
Worcester Warriors	16	3	1	12	255	345	27	33	0	6	20
Leeds Carnegie	15	1	0	14	233	482	24	60	0	2	6

Sale Sharks 22 – 16 Gloucester Rugby

Kick off 7.45pm Friday 14 March 2008
Attendance 9,266 : D Pearson referee

SALE SHARKS

15. B Foden 14. E Seveali'i 13. L McAlister 12. C Bell 11. O Ripol Fortuny 10. C Hodgson 9. S Martens 1. L Faure 2. S Bruno 3. S Turner 4. I Fernandez Lobbe 5. S Cox 6. C Jones 7. J Ma Fernandez Lobbe 8. S Chabal

Replacements

16. N Briggs 17. E Roberts 18. D Schofield 19. M Lund 20. W Cliff 21. L Thomas 22. C Mayor

GLOUCESTER RUGBY

15. J Bailey 14. C Sharples 13. L Lloyd 12. A Allen 11. M Foster 10. W Walker 9. G Cooper 1. N Wood 2. A Titterrell 3. J Forster 4. D Tuohy 5. W James 6. P Buxton 7. A Hazell 8. A Qera

Replacements

16. J Paul 17. C Califano 18. J Pendlebury 19. L Narraway 20. M Prendergast 21. R Lamb 22. H Trinder

We could not win the match but we did salvage a losing bonus point making it six in a week. How important that statistic is remains to be seen. But it is an achievement in itself when you consider how much we were up against it with two eighteen year-olds in the shape of Sharples and Trinder and the likes of Lamby, Allen and Foster counting as the seasoned professionals against what was to all intents and purposes, Sale's full-strength team. Couple that with the fact that the Edgeley Park pitch looked more like an abandoned allotment than a Premiership rugby playing surface, and you can see how difficult our task actually was.

Obviously the Gloucester hard men Buxton, James and Hazell managed to subdue Sale's physical approach to the game and Califano was outstanding.

New boy Dan Tuohy got himself sin-binned in the second half and Sale racked up ten points in his absence. Had that not happened there is a strong argument for the proposition that Gloucester would have won this match. But we all know the old saying about "if" and "your auntie", don't we? As it happened, Gloucester drew the short straw to bring Sale's losing run to an end.

However you look at it, Hodgson was the real source of our undoing with a personal tally of seventeen points accrued by way of one conversion, four penalties and a drop goal, even though Gloucester opened the scoresheet in minute six with a Willie Walker penalty to put Gloucester in the lead at Sale Sharks 0 – 3 Gloucester Rugby. It was the only time in the match that we were to be ibn front on the scoreboard.

Two minutes later Hodgson pegged our lead back to a level game at Sale Sharks 3 – 3 Gloucester Rugby, followed by a second six minutes later to put his side in the lead at Sale Sharks 6 – 3 Gloucester Rugby. From this point in the match we never headed Sale again.

Jeremy Paul came on as blood replacement for Andy Titterrell for a six minute period and then, in the twenty fourth minute, Hodgson claimed his third penalty to push his side even further ahead at Sale Sharks 9 – 3 Gloucester Rugby.

Willie Walker failed with a couple of long-distance penalty shots before slotting one over in the fortieth minute to pull three points back, and the largely uneventful first half came to an end at Sale Sharks 9 – 6 Gloucester Rugby.

Half time score Sale Sharks 9 – 6 Gloucester Rugby

The game slowly came to life in the second half. Two minutes in Hodgson added another penalty to his tally, taking the score to Sale Sharks 12 – 6 Gloucester Rugby and five minutes later Tuohy was yellow-carded for killing the ball.

On forty nine minutes Hodgson dropped a thirty-metre goal and on fifty four minutes a long Hodgson pass found Foden coming through on the burst. He crossed our line for a try after concerted Sale attacks just wore us down with their extra man. At Sale Sharks 17 – 6 Gloucester Rugby Hodgson converted a difficult kick from the touch line giving his side a thirteen points lead at Sale Sharks 19 – 6 Gloucester Rugby.

On fifty four minutes Sharples was replaced by Ryan Lamb who came on at standoff, and three minutes later Walker hauled us three points closer at Sale Sharks 19 – 9 Gloucester Rugby with another Gloucester penalty. At this point Narraway came on for Qera and six minutes later Prendergast replaced Cooper and Trinder came on for Leon Lloyd.

On sixty six minutes Paul replaced Titterrell and on seventy five minutes Califano replaced Nick Wood at loosehead and Jonathan Pendlebury came on for Dan Tuohy.

Chris Jones was yellow-carded right at the end of normal time for coming in at the side and we were awarded a penalty try when Sale collapsed at the third time of asking.

Walker nailed the conversion with the last kick of the game to put us only

six points behind and claim the losing bonus point at Sale Sharks 22 – 16 Gloucester Rugby.

SALE SHARKS	GLOUCESTER RUGBY
Try: Foden	**Try:** PENALTY
Conversion: Hodgson	**Conversion:** Walker
Penalty Goal: Hodgson (4)	**Penalty Goal:** Walker (3)

OTHER RESULTS
Leicester Tigers 36 - 23 Saracens
Worcester Warriors 10 - 10 Leeds Carnegie
Harlequins 22 - 16 Bath Rugby
London Irish 16 - 22 London Wasps
Newcastle Falcons 8 - 28 Bristol Rugby

CLUB	P	W	D	L	F	A	TF	TA	TB	LB	P
Gloucester Rugby	17	11	0	6	426	306	48	31	5	6	55
Leicester Rugby	17	11	0	6	420	308	42	25	4	4	52
Bath Rugby	16	1	0	5	380	288	42	26	5	2	51
Saracens	16	10	0	6	333	279	28	27	3	3	46
Harlequins	16	9	0	7	355	343	39	39	4	5	45
Saracens	17	9	0	8	377	353	35	34	1	5	42
London Wasps	15	8	2	5	363	314	37	32	3	3	42
London Irish	16	8	0	8	303	314	27	30	1	4	37
Bristol Rugby	16	7	1	8	298	314	31	31	3	2	34
Newcastle Falcons	15	6	0	9	240	337	24	36	1	2	27
Worcester Warriors	17	3	2	12	265	355	29	34	0	6	22
Leeds Carnegie	16	1	1	14	243	492	25	62	0	2	8

Worcester Warriors 17 – 14 Gloucester Rugby

kick off 3.00pm Saturday 29th March 2008
Attendance 10,197 : S Davey referee

WORCESTER WARRIORS
15. T Delport 14. M Garvey 13. D Rasmussen 12. S Tuitupou 11. M Benjamin 10. S Drahm 9. M Powell 1. T Windo 2. A Lutui 3. T Taumoepeau 4. G Rawlinson 5. C Gillies 6. T Wood 7. P Sanderson 8. K Horstmann

Replacements
16. D Morris 17. M Mullan 18. W Bowley 19. D Hickey 20. J Carlisle 21. J Arr 22. R Gear

GLOUCESTER RUGBY
15. O Morgan 14. I Balshaw 13. J Simpson-Daniel 12. A Allen 11. L Vainikolo 10. R Lamb 9. R Lawson 1. N Wood 2. A Titterrell 3. C Nieto 4. M Bortolami 5. A Brown 6. A Strokosch 7. A Qera 8. L Narraway

Replacements
16. J Paul 17. A Dickinson 18. W James 19. G Delve 20. G Cooper 21. C Paterson 22. W Walker

This match gave Worcester their first league win over Gloucester. Ironically it came through a last minute try by ex-Gloucester player Thinus Delport who slid across our line for a try so late in the match that the ref blew for full time directly the conversion attempt was taken.

It was our sixth successive away loss and it is a mystery how we engineered it, having controlled the game for the last hour, following a fairly unsteady starting twenty minutes. We controlled it in possession and territory but somehow – the dreadful weather conditions perhaps – we failed to take advantage of our superiority and our inability to close out the match finally cost us dear.

As expected, Worcester came out of the starting blocks at full tilt and with only two minutes gone they were on the scoreboard with a try after we turned over possession to them. Sanderson collected the ball and passed to centre Tuitupou who screamed over our line to touch down under the posts.

At Worcester Warriors 5 – 0 Gloucester Rugby, Drahm added the conversion and our hosts were off to a flying start.

Twenty minutes later they scored again when Marcel Garvey chased a Delport kick ahead to put Benjamin clear. This time Drahm missed the conversion and the score remained unchanged at Worcester Warriors 12 – 0 Gloucester Rugby.

Gloucester gradually played themselves back into the match, though. Qera was always dangerous, turning over possession on the ground and Narraway continually took the ball over the gainline. Meanwhile Alex Brown robbed Worcester blind at their own lineout.

Ten minutes later, with our first real opportunity of the match, we scored a memorable try when Balshaw took the ball deep into Worcester territory. As the ball returned, Lawson passed to Allen who found Simpson-Daniel in support on his shoulder. Sinbad got his pass to Big Les who bounced Delport and Garvey out of his way to cross their line for his eighth try of the season. Ryan Lamb duly obliged with the conversion and at Worcester Warriors 12 – 7 Gloucester Rugby, it was game on.

Garvey was clearly injured in his attempted tackle on Vainikolo and he was taken off the pitch. Gloucester continued to run the game and eight minutes later we scored our second try when Lawson darted through a gap and touched down. Again, Lamb added the conversion and we went in for the break at Worcester Warriors 12 – 14 Gloucester Rugby.

Half time score Worcester Warriors 12 – 14 Gloucester Rugby

The second half never lived up to the promise of the first half. Both packs of forwards fiercely contested every set piece and the backs tried to kick for position but neither side looked like scoring.

Paterson replaced Balshaw early in the half and on fifty nine minutes Cooper replaced Lawson and Delve replaced Strokosch.

With eighteen minutes of the match remaining Willie Walker came on for Ryan Lamb and he sought to pin Worcester down in their own half. But the home side defended valiantly and their reward came in the dying seconds when the play went from end-to-end and Gloucester, who had been pressing

Worcester's line, were forced to watch Delport cross their line and steal the match for the home side.

Benjamin sent an overhead pass to Delport who was unmarked out on the left and the match was over. Drahm missed his conversion attempt but the referee blew for time and at Worcester Warriors 7 – 14 Gloucester Rugby, the conversion hardly mattered.

WORCESTER WARRIORS
Try: Benjamin, Delport, Tuitupou
Conversion: Drahm

GLOUCESTER RUGBY
Try: Lawson, Vainikolo
Conversion: Lamb (2)

OTHER RESULTS
Sale Sharks 22 - 6 Bath Rugby
Leicester Tigers 19 - 24 London Wasps
Harlequins 15 - 9 Newcastle Falcons
London Irish 28 - 8 Bristol Rugby
Saracens 66 - 7 Leeds Carnegie

CLUB	P	W	D	L	F	A	TF	TA	TB	LB	P
Gloucester Rugby	18	11	0	7	440	323	50	34	5	7	56
Bath Rugby	18	12	0	6	405	326	44	28	5	2	55
Harlequins	18	11	0	7	398	367	43	41	5	5	54
Leicester Tigers	18	11	0	7	439	332	43	28	4	5	53
Sale	17	11	0	6	355	285	29	27	3	3	50
Saracens	18	10	0	8	443	360	45	35	2	5	47
London Wasps	16	9	2	5	387	333	40	33	3	3	46
London Irish	18	9	0	9	347	341	31	33	1	5	42
Bristol Rugby	18	7	1	10	321	370	34	38	3	2	34
Newcastle Falcons	17	6	0	11	264	368	26	37	1	4	29
Worcester Warriors	18	4	2	12	282	369	32	36	0	6	26
Leeds Carnegie	18	2	1	15	266	573	27	74	0	2	12

Heineken Cup
Quarter Final
Gloucester Rugby 3 – 16 Munster
Kingsholm
kick off 5.30pm Saturday 5 April 2008
Attendance 16,500 : N Owens (Wales) referee

GLOUCESTER RUGBY

15. O Morgan 14. C Paterson 13. J Simpson-Daniel 12. A Allen 11. L Vainikolo 10. R Lamb 9. R Lawson 1. N Wood 2. A Titterrell 3. C Nieto 4. M Bortolami 5. A Brown 6. P Buxton 7. A Hazell 8. L Narraway

Replacements

16. J Paul 17. A Dickinson 18. W James 19. G Delve 20. G Cooper 21. W Walker 22. M Tindall

MUNSTER

15. D Hurley 14. D Howlett 13. R Tipoki 12. L Mafi 11. I Dowling 10. R O'Gara 9. T O'Leary 1. T Buckley 2. J Flannery 3. J Hayes 4. D O'Callaghan 5. P O'Connell 6. A Quinlan 7. D Wallace 8. D Leamy

Replacements

16. F Sheahan 17. F Pucciariello 18. M O'Driscoll 19. A Foley 20. P Stringer 21. P Warwick 22. K Lewis

Most of Kingsholm Road and a large part of Worcester Street were closed for the afternoon as Munster supporters moved in and tried to drink the town dry. Gary Teague must have been rubbing his hands together like Fagin or Shylock as pint after pint of the black stuff was bought and consumed, bought and consumed, as the afternoon progressed. But all good things must come to an end and although the home support manfully matched the visitors pint for pint, the time finally came to abandon the streets and get into the stadium.

At our expense Munster proceeded to the semi finals with a three points to sixteen win over us at Kingsholm. We had our chances. For instance, in the first twenty minutes we had three eminently kickable penalty attempts but Chris Paterson, after a perfect display of place kicking in the 2007 World Cup and the Six Nations, failed with all three attempts. Our hearts sank. He was only on the pitch to kick goals for us. If he could not accomplish that for us, we were going to need someone else playing out wide.

In comparison with Paterson, O'Gara was on song with his place kicking right from the off. When Nieto got himself sin-binned after thirteen minutes O'Gara lost no time in putting his team three points ahead with his first attempt at goal. As our spirits sank, so Munster supporters' spirits soared.

Our first chance came after a mere eight seconds when Mafi fouled Olly Morgan. It was a sitter directly in front of the posts; Paterson missed it and the Kingsholm silence was deafening.

Five minutes later Big Les inadvertently went in late on Tipoki who expressed his disapproval in the time-honoured fashion. Lesley met like with like and soon there was a free-for-all of angry, punching players which gladdened the hearts of both sets of supporters. Referee Nigel Owens had no option but to stamp his authority on the afternoon's proceedings and warned both captains.

As luck would have it, Gloucester were the first to infringe after the referee's friendly advice when Carlos Nieto failed to roll away from a ruck and got ten minutes in the bin for his trouble. O'Gara slotted the ensuing penalty to put his team in the lead at Gloucester Rugby 0 – 3 Munster and from that point on the lead never changed hands.

Try as we might, Gloucester could not find the key to Munster's impervious defensive systems and three minutes from the end of the half the visitors struck a telling blow with a telling score at a telling point in the match. Gloucester were pressing their line with scrummage after scrummage but the ball was lost in contact and the Irishmen turned their implacable defence into an irresistible attack of their own. Seamlessly stringing together fourteen phases in a passage of play which lasted over two minutes they finally sent winger Ian Dowling over for an uncontested try.

At Gloucester Rugby 0 – 8 Munster, O'Gara showed he was fallible when he missed the conversion and Deano decided we needed some more muscle in our backline as he replaced Anthony Allen with Mike Tindall and Bucko was temporarily replaced by Gareth Delve as he went off for treatment.

Half time score Gloucester Rugby 0 – 8 Munster

Bucko returned to the fray one minute into the half but not even he could loosen Munster's stranglehold on the match.

The rain started, it was as icy cold as Munster's concentration and did nothing whatsoever to help our cause.

Eight minutes into the half O'Gara knocked over another penalty to move the score on to Gloucester Rugby 0 – 11 Munster which put us more or less at their mercy. Forcing us to chase the game; a situation which Munster love to be in, being past masters at the art of biding their time in defence and then launching a devastating counter-attack.

A predictable raft of Gloucester substitutions took place. Bucko went off again and Delve replaced him. Paul came on for Titterrell who needed attention, Will James replaced Bortolami and Walker came on for Paterson.

Six minutes later Titterrell was back on and as the sixty second minute
ticked by, Munster scored their second try of the afternoon.

Once more it came from a turnover in Munster territory. O'Callaghan gained possession and passed to Howlett who passed to Hurley the fullback. Hurley put in a sweetly-judged kick for Howlett to chase. He won the footrace to the corner and in a blur of arms and legs Howlett gathered the ball, dived for the line and touched down, all in a single fluid movement.

At Gloucester Rugby 0 – 16 Munster, O'Gara missed the conversion and there were more Gloucester replacements as Dickinson came on for Wood and Cooper replaced Lawson. With fourteen minutes to go Lamby knocked over a penalty but it was too little and too late. A converted try, and nothing less was the only score which would have put us back into the match with a fighting chance. Still, a measly three points on the board beats a whitewashing at your home ground, any time. Thus did our season show the first signs of stalling and it happened at Kingsholm which somehow makes it even harder to swallow.

On the day we were probably beaten by the better team, although Munster seemed to be working the officials brilliantly, especially when playing in offside positions for which they were rarely blown up. For all that, we did have a three to one advantage in the penalty count but could not make it tell on the scoreboard.

As for Munster, it is a matter for the record books that they went on to win the Heineken Cup and everybody in Gloucester was very happy for their success...

GLOUCESTER RUGBY
Penalty Goal: Lamb

MUNSTER
Try: Dowling, Howlett
Penalty Goal: O'Gara (2)

Gloucester Rugby 39 – 15 Saracens
Kickoff 3.00pm Saturday 12 April 2008
Attendance 12,300 : R Debney referee

GLOUCESTER RUGBY
15. W Walker 14. I Balshaw 13. J Simpson-Daniel 12. M Tindall 11. L Vainikolo 10. R Lamb 9. R Lawson 1. N Wood 2. A Titterrell 3. C Nieto 4. M Bortolami 5. A Brown 6. A Strokosch 7. A Qera 8. L Narraway

Replacements
16. O Azam 17. J Forster 18. W James 19. G Delve 20. G Cooper 21. C Paterson 22. J Adams

SARACENS
15. R Haughton 14. D Scarbrough 13. K Sorrell 12. A Powell 11. K Ratuvou 10. G Jackson 9. N de Kock 1. M Aguero 2. M Cairns 3. C Visagie 4. H Vyvyan 5. T Ryder 6. K Chesney 7. D Barrell 8. B Skirving

Replacements
16. F Ongaro 17. C Johnston 18. I Fullarton 19. D Seymour 20. M Rauluni 21. G Ross 22. R Penney

Rugby is a pitiless mistress. How else could a team with all the promise, class, creativity and style of Gloucester be out of the European adventure while an outfit of perennial under-achievers like Saracens get a quarter-final win against Ospreys to put them into the semi final of Europe? Sixth place in the Premiership and in the European semi – where's the justice?

So it was reassuring after Gloucester's disappointment the previous week against Munster, to reinforce our place at the top of the Premiership with an exhibition of controlled rugby and an impressive six-try scoreline in front of the home crowd.

We were totally dominant in the forwards. Ryan Lamb ran the show like a seasoned pro, scoring a fine brace of tries for his personal tally in the process.

On the negative side, we were more than capable of scoring more and, worryingly, we allowed Saracens to score two tries in injury time. But for all that, Saracens were outclassed by a team with five changes from the outfit which faced Munster the previous week. Including the return of Mike Tindall, making his first appearance since suffering an appalling liver injury in January in the Six Nations match against Wales, but there was no place for Chris Paterson who missed three early penalty attempts against Munster the previous week. His place on the left wing was taken by Ian Balshaw.

We were taken by surprise in the opening round when Dan Scarbrough made a break through the centre following a dummy run by Haughton which opened the gap for him. We would have been in trouble but for his pass going forward on its way to Ratuvou.

Gloucester opened the scoring after twelve minutes when Simpson-Daniel crossed their line following a well-constructed try that involved some excellent handling and some destructive bursts. First Qera made good use of some poor quality possession from a scrum. Bortolami and Tindall kept the dynamism going and Lamb moved the ball to the left for Willie Walker who delivered the scoring pass to Sinbad. The conversion from the touchline was not the easiest of kicks but Lamb knocked it over without hesitation and Gloucester were up and running at Gloucester Rugby 7 – 0 Saracens.

Five minutes later we struck again. Once more Lamb threw a long pass to Walker out on the wing and when the ball came back Big Les was there to add his seventeen and a half stone to the cause which significantly dismayed the Saracens defence and gave Balshaw sufficient space to get a long pass to Qera down the blindside who crossed for the score. This time we could not convert from wide out and shortly after – at Gloucester Rugby 12 – 0 Saracens Lamby went off for treatment to be temporarily replaced by Chris Paterson.

With twenty seven minutes gone Saracens opened their account with a penalty after a period of pressure in which their big forwards Vyvyan and Skirving were prominent. The penalty was converted by Jackson to put the score at Gloucester Rugby 12 – 3 Saracens and then, right on half time, Lamb – who had returned to the fray after six minutes' treatment – slotted a penalty to give us back our twelve points lead.

Half time score Gloucester Rugby 15 – 3 Saracens

The first fifteen minutes of the second half more or less sealed

179

our victory when Lamby scored his brace of tries, both resulting from Saracens mistakes.

With a matter of three minutes gone he fielded a very poor attempt at a clearance kick by de Kock, bursting through the defence he stepped away from Vyvyan like a matador, sidestepped Haughton and touched down for a great example of an individual try. He cockily rubbed salt into Saracens wounds by adding the conversion to move the score to Gloucester Rugby 22 – 3 Saracens.

If Saracens were going to stand any chance whatsoever in the match they needed to score next but it was not to be; again it was at the expense of de Kock four minutes after the previous try. This time from a lineout near the Gloucester twenty two.

Saracens won possession and de Kock sent out his pass which was read perfectly by Lamby who intercepted and set off for the Saracens line with winger Haughton in hot pursuit all in vain. Lamb scored his second try and added the conversion too, to put Saracens out of the game at Gloucester Rugby 29 – 3 Saracens.

Azam and Forster came on as replacements for Titterrell and Nieto, respectively and we kept our foot down to the metal. Our next score came fifteen minutes into the half. It came from an attack covering all of sixty metres and involving at least six Gloucester players. We turned over possession following a number of short-range Saracens drives and Lawson sent down a cross kick for Balshaw to chase. Delve got involved, then Qera who creamed the defending Haughton and from the breakdown they moved the ball to the left.

Lamb moved the ball to Simpson-Daniel, who had Walker supporting on his shoulder and when the ball got to Vainikolo the real damage was done. Scarbrough bounced off him and landed square on his buttocks with a visible wince that delighted the Shedheads. Meanwhile Big Les set off for the tryline with firm intentions. We could not add the conversion but at Gloucester Rugby 34 - 3 Saracens it was hardly a matter of supreme importance.

Two minutes later a cross kick from Lamb should have resulted in a fairly straight forward try for Balshaw but inexplicably he elected to tap the ball back for Bortolami who was unable to hold it and the chance went begging.

One minute short of the hour mark Saracens lock, Ryder, was yellow-carded and another score was inevitable as they were reduced to fourteen men. It was not long in coming. Within two minutes Lawson scored a first-phase try (still a rarity in the Premiership) when he broke down the blindside from a scrum to touch down near the corner. The conversion attempt went astray again but Lawson's try – which put the score at Gloucester Rugby 39 – 3 Saracens – meant we had scored twenty four unanswered points in twenty five minutes. Awesome.

Going into the final fifteen minutes Cooper replaced Lawson and Will James came on for Qera. But we still eased up and gave our visitors a couple of soft chances to make the scoreline look better for them.

First Powell finished off a move for Ross to convert, putting the score at Gloucester Rugby 39 – 10 Saracens. Then Skirving touched down in the final play of the match from a crosskick by Ross which remained unconverted and the match finished at Gloucester Rugby 39 – 15 Saracens.

With Leeds coming to Kingsholm the following week it was looking more and more like a home advantage in the playoffs semi final for us.

GLOUCESTER RUGBY
Try: Lamb (2), Lawson, Qera, S-Daniel, Vainikolo
Conversion: Lamb (3)
Penalty Goal: Lamb

SARACENS
Try: Powell, Skirving
Conversion: Ross
Penalty Goal: Jackson

OTHER RESULTS
Bristol Rugby 17 - 24 Sale Sharks
London Wasps 49 - 12 Worcester Warriors
Leeds Carnegie 6 - 32 Harlequins
Newcastle Falcons 8 - 13 London Irish
London Wasps 29 - 19 Sharks
Bath Rugby 26 - 12 Leicester Tigers

CLUB	P	W	D	L	F	A	TF	TA	TB	LB	P
Gloucester Rugby	19	12	0	7	479	338	56	36	6	7	61
Harlequins	19	12	0	7	430	373	47	41	6	5	59
Bath Rugby	18	12	0	6	405	326	44	28	5	2	55
Sale Sharks	18	12	0	6	379	302	32	29	3	3	54
Leicester Tigers	18	11	0	7	439	332	43	28	4	5	53
London Wasps	17	10	2	5	436	345	47	35	4	3	51
Saracens	19	10	0	9	458	399	47	41	2	5	47
London Irish	19	10	0	9	360	349	33	34	1	5	46
Bristol Rugby	19	7	1	11	338	394	36	41	3	3	35
Newcastle Falcons	18	6	0	12	272	381	27	39	1	5	30
Worcester Warriors	19	4	2	13	294	418	34	43	0	6	26
Leeds Carnegie	19	2	1	16	272	605	27	78	0	2	12

Gloucester Rugby 39 – 16 Leeds Carnegie

kick off 3.00pm Saturday 19 April 2008
Attendance 11,753 : referee M Fox

GLOUCESTER RUGBY

15. W Walker 14. I Balshaw 13. J Simpson-Daniel 12. M Tindall 11. L Vainikolo 10. R Lamb 9. G Cooper 1. A Dickinson 2. O Azam 3. C Nieto 4. W James 5. M Bortolami 6. A Strokosch 7. A Qera 8. G Delve

Replacements

16. A Titterrell 17. J Forster 18. A Brown 19. P Buxton 20. R Lawson 21. C Paterson 22. O Morgan

LEEDS CARNEGIE

15. L Hinton 14. S Armstrong 13. R Vickerman 12. L Burrell 11. J Holtby 10. A di Bernardo 9. J Bedford 1. M MacDonald 2. J Parkes 3. F Pala'amo 4. P Bouza 5. S Hooper 6. R Oakley 7. C Clark 8. M Lock

Replacements

16. A Hopcroft 17. V Ma'asi 18. E Lund 19. K Myall 20. D Edwards 21. J Brooks 22. J Goodridge

Another wet day at Kingsholm and another victory for Gloucester sent Leeds back to National League One for the upcoming season. We earned the bonus point (for the second week in succession) to help guarantee a home match in the play-offs and Leeds can no longer catch Worcester Warriors so their stay in the Premiership will be limited to one season.

It was a straightforward matter of dominating possession and territory. We were just too strong for them. Too strong physically and too strong in terms of the team as a whole.

Qera reaped his just rewards, scoring a hat-trick of tries. His first came thirteen minutes into the game when Delve picked up from the base of a scrum and linked up with his Wales squad mate Gareth Cooper. A couple of rucks followed and

Qera took up a position outside Lamb, took the pass and drove for the line, crossing near the post leaving Lamb with an easy enough conversion to put the score at Gloucester Rugby 7 – 0 Leeds Carnegie.

Leeds battled on gamely enough and although a rout was inevitable, they twice got to within a single point of our score. First they scored a penalty through di Bernardo on the quarter hour when we were deemed to be offside at a ruck. Gloucester Rugby 7 – 3 Leeds Carnegie, which became Gloucester Rugby 7 – 6 Leeds Carnegie on twenty minutes when the Argentinian stand off landed a second penalty.

Three minutes later a Lamb penalty put us four points ahead at Gloucester Rugby 10 – 6 Leeds Carnegie but the Leeds player would not be denied and responded with a drop goal three minutes later to put his side within a point again. This time at Gloucester Rugby 10 – 9 Leeds Carnegie.

Our breakthrough came in the twenty eighth minute. Strokosch took a lineout ball at the tail and it was moved to Tindall in the centre who cleverly off loaded to Qera in the tackle who took off through a defensive gap at a rate of knots.

Gloucester forwards arrived in swarms at the breakdown fifteen metres from Leeds' line. The ball was moved closer and closer and it fell to Azam to score the try next to the posts to give us a 15 – 9 lead. Lamb added the conversion and the score stood at Gloucester Rugby 17 – 9 Leeds Carnegie. Delve was left requiring treatment from this passage of play and he was temporarily replaced by Pete Buxton on twenty eight minutes.

Five minutes later a fight erupted between second row opponents Will James and Leeds' captain Stuart Hooper. A traditional free-for-all ensued, resulting in Jamer and Hooper cooling their heels in the sin bin for the rest of the half. Meanwhile, Delve returned to the pitch and Bucko trotted off and the score stayed the same until half time.

Half time score Gloucester Rugby 17 – 9 Leeds Carnegie

Titterrell replaced Azam and Paterson came on for Vainikolo then ten minutes into the half Leeds were ajudged offside and Lamb added the three penalty points to put us eleven points clear at Gloucester Rugby 20 – 9 Leeds Carnegie and one minute later he added insult to injury again, when di Bernardo was fatally slow with his pass and Lamb took full advantage for his second interception try in two weeks, racing home unchallenged to increase our lead to Gloucester Rugby 25 – 9 Leeds Carnegie.

As the hour mark approached Ma'asi was yellow-carded for obstructing Will James and Gloucester turned up the intensity in the search for the four-try bonus point. Buxton replaced Strokosch and two minutes later Qera scored his second try of the day two minutes later when we drove a lineout forward. Bortolami peeled off and made the hard yards and Qera smacked through the last of the Leeds defence to touch down alongside the posts. Lamb converted and at Gloucester Rugby 32 – 9 Leeds Carnegie, there was no looking back.

Twelve minutes from time Qera crossed for his third try. This time it was a short-range effort, burrowing over from a ruck on Leeds' line. Lamby added the conversion and moved the score on to Gloucester Rugby 39 – 9 Leeds Carnegie.

Three minutes from time Bortolami was sin-binned for obstructing in a lineout and credit to Leeds, they took advantage of their superiority of numbers two minutes from time when replacement Edwards scrambled over the line from close-up to put the score at Gloucester Rugby 39 – 14 Leeds Carnegie. Brooks ended the match – and Leeds' short stay in the Premiership - with a conversion to close the match at Gloucester Rugby 39 – 16 Leeds Carnegie.

GLOUCESTER RUGBY
Try: Azam, Lamb, Qera (3)
Conversion: Lamb (4)
Penalty Goal: Lamb (2)

LEEDS CARNEGIE
Try: Edwards
Conversion: Brooks
Penalty Goal: di Bernardo (2)

OTHER RESULTS
London Irish 13 - 6 Harlequins
Leicester Tigers 32 - 14 Bristol Rugby
Worcester Warriors 20 - 23 Bath Rugby
Saracens 29 - 40 London Wasps
Sale Sharks 53 - 10 Newcastle Falcons

CLUB	P	W	D	L	F	A	TF	TA	TB	LB	P
Gloucester Rugby	20	13	0	7	518	354	61	37	7	7	66
Bath Rugby	20	14	0	6	454	358	50	33	5	2	63
London Wasps	19	12	2	5	505	393	55	41	5	3	60
Harlequins	20	12	0	8	436	386	47	42	6	6	60
Sale Sharks	20	13	0	7	451	341	41	32	4	3	59
Leicester Tigers	20	12	0	8	483	372	50	33	5	5	58
London Irish	20	11	0	9	373	355	34	34	1	5	50
Saracens	20	10	0	10	487	439	52	47	3	5	48
Bristol Rugby	20	7	1	12	352	426	38	46	3	3	35
Newcastle Falcons	19	6	0	13	282	434	28	47	1	5	30
Worcester Warriors	20	4	0	14	314	441	37	46	0	7	27
Leeds Carnegie	20	2	1	17	288	644	28	83	0	2	12

On Saturday 3 May Gloucester Rugby's rightful place at the top of the table was usurped by our neighbours and favoured sparring-partners, Bath Rugby, when they beat Saracens by 66 points to 21 in their Round 21 match to give them 68 league points.

CLUB	P	W	D	L	F	A	TF	TA	TB	LB	P
Bath Rugby	21	15	0	6	520	379	59	36	6	2	68
Gloucester Rugby	20	13	0	7	518	354	61	37	7	7	66
London Wasps	19	12	2	5	505	393	55	41	5	3	66
Harlequins	20	12	0	8	436	386	47	42	6	6	60
Sale Sharks	20	13	0	7	451	341	41	32	4	3	59
Leicester Tigers	20	12	0	8	483	372	50	33	5	5	58
London Irish	20	11	0	9	373	355	34	34	1	5	50
Saracens	21	10	0	11	508	505	55	56	3	5	48
Bristol Rugby	21	7	1	13	373	448	38	49	3	4	36
Worcester Warriors	21	5	2	14	336	462	40	46	0	7	31
Newcastle Falcons	19	6	0	13	282	434	28	47	1	5	30
Leeds Carnegie	20	2	1	17	288	644	28	83	0	2	12

London Wasps 17 – 25 Gloucester Rugby

Kick off 3.00pm Sunday 4 May 2008
Attendance 10,000 : referee W Barnes

LONDON WASPS

15. J Lewsey 14. P Sackey 13. F Waters 12. R Flutey 11. T Voyce 10. D Cipriani 9. E Reddan 1. T French 2. R Ibanez 3. T Payne 4. S Shaw 5. T Palmer 6. J Worsley 7. T Rees 8. L Dallaglio

Replacements

16. J Ward 17. M Holford 18. G Skivington 9. J Haskell 20. M McMillan 21. M van Gisbergen 22. J Staunton

GLOUCESTER RUGBY

15. O Morgan 14. I Balshaw 13. M Tindall 12. A Allen 11. J Simpson-Daniel 10. R Lamb 9. R Lawson 1. N Wood 2. A Titterrell 3. C Nieto 4. M Bortolami 5. A Brown 6. A Strokosch 7. A Qera 8. L Narraway

Replacements

16. O Azam 17. A Dickinson 18. W James 19. P Buxton 20. G Delve 21. G Cooper 22. W Walker

The current champions of Europe, with an eight-long winning sequence to their credit came second on their home pitch to a Gloucester side with a point to prove. We took an early lead and although Wasps threatened, a second half try put paid to their chances. Wasps had a mid week fixture to fulfil against Newcastle Falcons, a hangover from their interrupted season, and if they failed to land maximum points it meant Gloucester would have a home fixture in the play-offs.

We were the last team to beat Wasps in the league, at Kingsholm on 26 January, but it was eighteen years since we beat them on their home turf in the league and we fancied our chances. We had not managed to overcome the Bath Recreation Ground jinx in our first match of the new year, but turning over Wasps at home would be a very welcome second choice.

Now, a quick glance at the bench was enough to show the travelling Shedheads that Deano was approaching the match with the intention of matching the home side in the physicality stakes. We knew we could handle them in the scrummages and we knew we could best them in attack but we needed to match them in broken field play, particularly at the tackle area, so we opted for five forwards among our seven replacements:

Two front rows, a second row, a utility back-five forward and an out and out back row player. Sound rugby sense there. This was a team that could turn over London Wasps all right.

Every Shedhead and Shedette in the land could hear the blood pounding in their ears whether they were at the match, watching it on TV, listening on the radio or following it on teletext. This was a big match and we were going to win it. We were going to win because it was Wasps. But a good start would be imperative. Give Wasps a lead and you are sunk before you have even broken sweat. The Wasps' game reflects their very season inasmuch as they will come back at you at the very end. When it should be all over they will continue to come at you. You can expect it, prepare for it and wait for it but you will still find it very, very hard to withstand it.

So scoring first was crucial and it was pretty to watch. Qera made inroads as he does. The ball came back to Lamby who put up a garryowen for Olly Morgan. Lewsey made the ball safe but Morgan tied him up with a textbook smother tackle which dislodged the ball and it was snaffled by Sinbad. He grabbed the ball and scooted over the line and behind the posts for our first try of the day with seven minutes gone. The conversion attempt failed, forcing a collective groan from Gloucester supporters everywhere but three minutes later we landed our second try of the day through Mike Tindall. We were handling their rush defence more than adequately, switching our point of attack and generally making life difficult for the home boys. A switch to the blindside by Lawson put Qera in space and he sent Balshaw off and galloping. Our second rows drove straight up the centre and when the ball came to Tindall he had the pace and strength to beat Paul Sackey to the line and there are not that many backs in the Premiership of whom you could say that. This time there was no mistake with Lamb's conversion and we were twelve points ahead without reply at London Wasps 0 – 12 Gloucester Rugby.

Wasps tried everything they knew to no avail. The Gloucester defence was solid and Cipriani did nothing to help his team's cause by missing two reasonable penalty attempts. But it was a case of third time lucky for him when he got his first penalty over in the twentieth minute. However it was a simple case of tit for tat as four minutes later Lamby slotted another penalty to put the score at London Wasps 3 – 15 Gloucester Rugby.

Two minutes later Gloucester took a heavy body blow when Nieto was yellow-cared for failing to roll away at a ruck. Predictably enough they kicked for the corner and the resultant catch-and-drive saw Ibanez peeling off the back to touch down. Cipriani duly added the conversion to put the score at London Wasps 10 – 15 Gloucester Rugby and that is how the score stayed for the rest of the half.

Half time score London Wasps 10 – 15 Gloucester Rugby

Gloucester made three substitutions in the first seven minutes: Dickinson
replaced Wood; Delve came on for Narraway and Azam substituted for Titterrell. Then, eight minutes into the half, we scored again. This time through Olly Morgan.

Lamb collared Cipriani – to a chorus of complaints about a high tackle – and Strokosch took possession. A kick from Lamb then took an unintended route as the ball came off the outside of his boot but Simpson-Daniel was sufficiently switched on to gather it perilously close to the touchline and ward off the attentions of Sackey long enough to get an elegant pass to Morgan who touched down, putting the scoreline at London Wasps 10 – 20 Gloucester Rugby. Lamb added the conversion and it was London Wasps 10 – 22 Gloucester Rugby going into the last half hour – always the most dangerous part of a match but particularly so when the opposition happens to be Wasps.

With twenty three minutes left Deano decided that we needed a bit more grunt and a bit less finesse from our second row and so Browner was replaced by Will James.

There was eighteen minutes of the match remaining when the inevitable occurred and Wasps came right back into the reckoning with a clever try by Ibanez – his second of the day.

Again Wasps were awarded a penalty and elected to kick for the corner but we stole their ball. Quite how we did that with Alex Brown off the park and on the bench remains a mystery but we did it. Unfortunately the ball went loose and the wily old campaigner Ibanez pounced on it for his second try of the day.

Staunton, who had replaced Cipriani by this time, added the conversion and at London Wasps 17 – 22 Gloucester Rugby, the stage was set for a grandstand finale.

The determination and courage shown by the Gloucester players was nothing short of phenomenal. The harder Wasps tried, and they certainly tried, the stronger the Gloucester resistance and the more resolute and composed the Gloucester team became.

When we gained possession we played the clock down with a series of short-range drives and it was well into injury time when Wasps were penalised for failing to roll away. Ryan Lamb strode up and nonchalantly slotted the penalty which robbed the home team of the losing bonus point. Perfect.

LONDON WASPS
Try: Ibanez (2)
Conversion: Cipriani, Staunton
Penalty Goal: Cipriani

GLOUCESTER RUGBY
Try: Morgan, S-Daniel, Tindall
Conversion: Lamb (2)
Penalty Goal: Lamb (2)

OTHER RESULTS
Bristol Rugby 21 - 22 Worcester Warriors
Bath Rugby 66 - 21 Saracens
Harlequins 16 - 23 Sale Sharks
London Irish 43 - 20 Leeds Carnegie
Newcastle Falcons 28 - 25 Leicester Tigers

CLUB	P	W	D	L	F	A	TF	TA	TB	LB	P
Gloucester Rugby	21	14	0	7	543	371	64	39	7	7	70
Bath Rugby	21	15	0	6	520	379	59	36	6	2	68
Sale Sharks	21	14	0	7	474	357	43	34	4	3	63
Harlequins	21	12	0	9	452	409	49	44	6	7	61
London Wasps	21	12	2	6	522	418	57	44	5	3	60
Leicester Tigers	21	12	0	9	508	400	53	36	5	6	59
London Irish	21	12	0	9	416	375	41	36	2	5	55
Saracens	21	10	0	11	508	505	55	56	3	5	48
Bristol Rugby	21	7	1	13	373	448	38	49	3	4	36
Newcastle Falcons	21	7	0	13	310	459	31	50	1	5	34
Worcester Warriors	21	5	2	14	336	462	40	46	0	7	31
Leeds Carnegie	21	2	1	18	308	687	30	90	0	2	12

Gloucester Rugby 8 – 6 Bath Rugby

Kick off 3.00pm Saturday 10 May 2008
Attendance 16,500 : referee D Pearson

GLOUCESTER RUGBY

15. I Balshaw 14. J Simpson-Daniel 13. M Tindall 12. A Allen 11. L Vainikolo 10. R Lamb 9. R Lawson 1. N Wood 2. A Titterrell 3. C Nieto 4. M Bortolami 5. A Brown 6. A Strokosch 7. A Qera 8. G Delve

Replacements

16. O Azam 17. A Dickinson 18. W James 19. L Narraway 20. G Cooper 21. W Walker 22. M Foster

BATH RUGBY

15. J Maddock 14. A Higgins 13. T Cheeseman 12. O Barkley 11. M Banahan 10. A James 9. M Claassens 1. D Flatman 2. L Mears 3. M Stevens 4. S Borthwick 5. D Grewcock 6. J Fa'amatuainu 7. M Lipman   8. D Browne

Replacements

16. P Dixon 17. D Bell 18. P Short 19. C Goodman 20. N Walshe 21. S Berne 22. A Crockett

What better way to end a Premiership season than with a derby match? What better way to end a season than a match against your neighbours to decide who will secure the league top spot?   And sitting in the stands watching every tackle, every pass, every angle and every scrum, the new England supremo Martin Johnson alongside Rob Andrew. As if the importance of the match were not sufficient, every player is now planning to put in the performance of his life in the hope of impressing Jonno sufficiently to pencil in his name on his list of probables and possibles.

However, the match itself never lived up to its promise as a spectacle. Neither team quite put together the running, passing game of which they are both more than capable. The game only produced a single try. And yet the match was everything you hoped it would be.

Commitment, physicality, relentless attack and unrelenting defence, what more could you ask for? The pace and intensity took its toll on everybody with three established England internationals – Gloucester's Tindall and Bath's Mears and Stevens - failing to go the distance. A bad sign for all of them with the 32-man touring side due to be announced the following week.

Surprisingly it was Bath who started the stronger of the two teams and it was only a last ditch tackle by Mike Tindall which saved a Bath try after only seven minutes when Barkley orchestrated a break down the centre.

But the attacking option did not belong exclusively to Bath. Balshaw's scintillating pace opened gaps in their defence and an inside pass to Tindall very nearly landed a try.

Shortly afterwards Barkley initiated another threatening attack from a scrum deep in their own half, sending Higgins away through a gap before feeding Banahan, their giant winger. It was Balshaw's turn to put in a courageous one-on-one try-saving tackle. It was his personal way of putting up two fingers to the many critics of his recent international displays.

Tindall's early departure from the pitch with an ankle injury, occurring in the fifteenth minute, could so easily have had a detrimental effect on the whole team but they kept their composure and shape and Willie Walker substituted admirably.

Two minutes after Tins' departure Gloucester scored the first points of the day through a 35-metre Lamb penalty, putting us ahead at Gloucester Rugby 3 - 0 Bath Rugby.

But it was still Bath who controlled possession and territory, a fact underlined at twenty five minutes when Stevens showed why he should be England's first-choice tighthead in front of Phil Vickery. He stampeded through the Gloucester defence on a beautifully-angled run, Lamby attempted the head on tackle and mercifully survived the experience, although he did bounce quite a distance before landing flat on his back. Stevens had scented the tryline and nothing was going to stop him reaching it.

It was only Simpson-Daniel's bravery that prevented a certain try. Sinbad hit the much heavier man with all the bad intent he could muster and not only stopped him dead in his tracks five metres out, but he also turned him in the tackle. There is never anything funny about rugby injuries, no matter who suffers them. So perhaps the appropriate word should be "ironic", rather than "funny". The ironic thing about this massive tackle by Sinbad on a bloke five stone heavier is that as a result Stevens had to be substituted a couple of minutes later.

Testament indeed to Simpson-Daniel's commitment to the cause.

In the meantime Barkley landed a penalty to level the scores at Gloucester Rugby 3 – 3 Bath Rugby.

On thirty four minutes Gloucester hit Bath with a dagger under the ribs, with due consideration to their superiority in just about every facet of the match.

Qera took Lawson's pass and made some inroads before shipping it on to Allen with a pass so delicate that it belied its deadliness. Allen duly found Willie Walker who is always alive to any possibility and he saw the chance for Simpson-Daniel. There was still plenty for him to accomplish before the try was scored but he demonstrated his strength which belies his size to break through two tackles before reaching the line.

The Gloucester support were quite pleased with this and politely acknowledged the fact that they were now in the lead by five points at Gloucester Rugby 8 – 3 Bath Rugby.

But pride comes before a fall and four minutes from the break Barkley landed his second penalty to put his side within two points at Gloucester Rugby 8 – 6 Bath Rugby.

Half time score Gloucester Rugby 8 – 6 Bath Rugby

We started the half with the predictable replacements: Azam for Titterrell; Dickinson for Wood while he received treatment and Narraway for Delve. Then with ten minutes to go Wood returned and Cooper replaced Lawson.

It was a half as brutal and beautiful as the first half had been. Bath attacked relentlessly, seeming to target Willie Walker in the centre and he resisted manfully as did Balshaw at fullback who never put a foot wrong.

With ten minutes to go Vainikolo found himself in possession and made some hard yards infield before shipping it on to Narraway who galloped over for the touchdown but the referee called play back to where he judged Ryan Lamb had thrown it forward at the start of the move. We were still two points in the lead. In the event the decision did not affect the outcome and we won by eight points to six and we had won the league. We were hoping against hope that we would meet them again at Twickenham where we had an old score to settle. Going back to the 1990 Pilkington Cup final when Bath hammered us off the park by 48 points to 6.

However, their losing bonus point was not enough to keep them second in the league and they were having to travel to Adams Park to meet London Wasps the following week. They

194

would have a hard job beating Wasps at home but they would be our preferred opponents in the final.

As for us, we were going to meet Leicester at Kingsholm for a four-thirty kickoff the following Sunday, secure in the knowledge that no team had won a Premiership play-off away from home.

GLOUCESTER RUGBY
Try: S-Daniel
Penalty Goal: Lamb

BATH RUGBY
Penalty Goal: Barkley (2)

OTHER RESULTS
Leeds Carnegie 28 - 45 London Wasps
Leicester Tigers 31 - 28 Harlequins
Sale Sharks 7 - 17 London Irish
Saracens 25 - 20 Bristol Rugby
Worcester Warriors 51 - 10 Newcastle Falcons

CLUB	P	W	D	L	F	A	TF	TA	TB	LB	P
Gloucester Rugby	22	15	0	7	551	377	65	39	7	7	74
London Wasps	22	14	2	6	599	459	67	49	7	3	70
Bath Rugby	22	15	0	7	526	387	59	37	6	3	69
Leicester Tigers	22	13	0	9	539	428	58	40	6	6	64
Sale Sharks	22	14	0	8	481	374	44	37	4	3	63
Harlequins	22	12	0	10	480	440	53	49	7	8	63
London Irish	22	13	0	9	433	382	44	37	2	5	59
Saracens	22	11	0	11	533	525	58	58	3	5	52
Bristol Rugby	22	7	1	14	393	473	40	52	3	5	37
Worcester Warriors	22	6	2	14	387	472	48	47	1	7	36
Newcastle Falcons	22	7	0	15	333	542	34	62	1	5	34
Leeds Carnegie	22	2	1	19	336	732	33	96	0	2	12

Gloucester Rugby 25 – 26 Leicester Tigers

Kick off 4.30pm Sunday 18 May 2008
Attendance 16,500 : referee W Barnes

GLOUCESTER RUGBY
15. W Walker 14. I Balshaw 13. J Simpson-Daniel 12. A Allen
11. L Vainikolo 10. R Lamb 9. R Lawson 1. N Wood 2. A
Titterrell 3. C Nieto 4. M Bortolami 5. A Brown 6. A Strokosch
7. A Qera 8. G Delve

Replacements
16. O Azam 17. J Forster 18. W James 19. L Narraway 20. M
Prendergast 21. J Adams 22. M Foster

LEICESTER TIGERS
15. G Murphy 14. T Varndell 13. D Hipkiss 12. A Mauger 11. A
Tuilagi 10. A Goode 9. H Ellis 1. B Stankovich 2. M Davies 3. J
White 4. M Wentzel 5. B Kay 6. M Corry 7. B Herring 8. J
Crane

Replacements
16. G Chuter 17. M Ayerza 18. R Blaze 19. T Croft 20. C
Laussucq 21. S Vesty 22. A Erinle

It always used to be Bath's Stuart Barnes who dropped a last-minute goal to rob us of victory. Home or away, it mattered not to Barnesey but he has long been retired and so it fell to Leicester's Andy Goode to replace him as the Kingsholm bogey man, dropping a goal in the dying seconds to rob us of a victory we had earned through blood, sweat and tears. It could not have been a more obvious mugging if Goode had worn a hoody and carried a knife. Not just a mugging either. Goode murdered our season for us. Kicking it to death in the last minute of the match and how are we ever going to recover from that?

Being a gracious loser is sometimes the hardest thing in sport and this time it was very, very hard. Team, club and supporters had been working towards this moment for six years. Building, planning, gritting our teeth at the setbacks firm in the knowledge that this young team would win the Premiership Championship for us one day, and then go on to achieve great things in Europe. But what can we do now? This is the team at its zenith. It has gone as far as it can and it was a step short of its goal, for had we beaten Leicester we would surely have gone on to ruin the Big Day Out of

Wasps and their pantomime villain captain, Lawrence Dallaglio.

Ideally we would have met Bath in the final. The older ones among us are still suffering the mental anguish of that 48 – 6 stuffing they inflicted on us at Twickenham on 5 May 1990.

At Twickenham for the Premiership final we would certainly have defeated them and been able to sleep soundly again. But no team has ever won a play-off match away from home and Bath proved to be no exception. They relinquished the field to London Wasps by 21 points to 10.

Still, Wasps would be nice second-choice opponents for us. They had ambushed us in our first final on 31 May 2003 when our only score came through a single Ludovic Mercier penalty against 39 points for them. Yes, Wasps would be very acceptable opponents at Twickenham in our third attempt at the Premiership Championship. But first there was the small consideration of getting past our semi final opposition, Leicester Tigers.

How difficult can it be to beat Leicester? A weakened, unconfident, inconsistent Leicester. A Leicester which at one point in the game was reduced to a rugby league team of thirteen players. How difficult can it be to put a wounded, miserable, aged Tiger out of its misery? A Leicester of whom even their coach and ex-playing stalwart Richard Cockerill had insisted they would win nothing "because they were not good enough". Well, at Kingsholm on 17 May 2008 beating Leicester was not difficult at all. No, it was an impossibility.

Had we wished to read it, the writing was probably on the wall before the kick off when Tindall limped off the pitch and took no further part in proceedings. His experience, playing skills and organisational ability were a keystone to our season and if he ever gets fully fit again he ought to be a shoo-in for the England captaincy.

The match started predictably enough. Lamby celebrated his twenty second birthday by knocking over a penalty at six minutes and Goode put his side level at eleven minutes, also with a penalty. Five minutes later Lamby put us ahead once more with his second penalty of the day at Gloucester Rugby 6 – 3 Leicester Tigers.

Ten minutes later Crane was yellow-carded for pulling back Simpson-Daniel – these new skin-tight players' jerseys were supposed to put an end to all that - and with less than a quarter of an hour to go to the break, we were looking comfortable enough and when Lamby kicked his third penalty two minutes later the Gloucester supporters were starting to smirk amongst themselves. How easy this was. Why had we been so nervous?

With five minutes to go to half time Harry Ellis got himself sent to the sin bin following a series of Leicester infringements and Lamby kicked another penalty two minutes from the end of the half to put us well ahead at Gloucester Rugby 12 – 3 Leicester Tigers.

Half time score Gloucester Rugby 12 – 3 Leicester Tigers

Leicester were at our mercy. There for the taking. We were seeking retribution for their humiliation of us at Twickenham in last year's final. Revenge was going to be oh, so sweet. But whether it was the change of end, giving Goode the wind at his back, whether it was their half time team talk, or whether they just remembered that they were Leicester, champions of Europe; whatever the reason, they came out for round two with much more strength of purpose than previously.

Two minutes into the half Goode struck with a penalty putting his side closer at Gloucester Rugby 12 – 6 Leicester Tigers but Lamb reintroduced the nine points difference at Gloucester Rugby 15 – 6 Leicester Tigers when he kicked a penalty at forty nine minutes at the same time as Narraway replaced Delve.

Then on fifty two minutes the first try of the day was scored. Leicester won a scrum in our half and Crane passed to Goode who threw out a wide and wonderful pass to Tuilagi who swatted off the attentions of three Gloucester tacklers as if they were nothing more than bothersome sand flies on the Samoan beaches of his birthplace before touching down in the corner. Goode added the difficult conversion and the score stood at a dangerous-looking Gloucester Rugby 15 – 13 Leicester Tigers. It was time for Simpson-Daniel to do what he does best.

On fifty seven minutes the chance presented itself. Lawson and Narraway combined on the left and got the ball to Qera who took it up at his very special pace. He came off his right foot to pass Tuilagi and drew the attentions of Geordan Murphy before finding Sinbad in support on his shoulder. This was a quality of play completely unexpected of Qera. We were used to seeing him making and taking the hits full on, unaware of his more subtle footballing skills which he displayed in this move.

Sinbad streaked over and gave Lamby the opportunity for a few more birthday points, which he gladly did and the scoreline read Gloucester Rugby 22 – 13 Leicester Tigers. Nine points ahead with twenty three minutes to go.

With sixty three minutes on the clock disaster struck. Geordan Murphy got possession deep in their half and took off like an Irish hare through the heart of Gloucester's defence. As he approached the halfway line Crane took it on for him. We recovered possession just outside our twenty two metres line through Lawson who found Lamb but we were uncharacteristically jumpy, perhaps the new-found determination in the Leicester team had negatively affected Gloucester. Whatever, Lamby's clearance came off the side of his boot and we were suddenly in trouble. Deep, deep trouble.

Balshaw gathered the ball. Did he think Willie would make a better job of clearing our lines? He attempted to pass to Walker who suddenly looked as if he had not read the situation at all and at the same time Balsh appeared to change his mind and instead of passing to Willie, he decided to pass to another supporting Gloucester defender standing even deeper.

This was not Balsh's greatest decision ever. The perceived defender was in fact our goalpost and we were in even deeper trouble! Meanwhile Mauger was closing in on this comedy of errors like the Angel of Death and as the ball bounced off the post Mauger took it nicely and fell over our line to score a try.

Kingsholm was speechless. Well, the Gloucester parts of it anyway. The Leicester supporters loudly showed their appreciation as their team came within four points of us at Gloucester Rugby 22 – 18 Leicester Tigers. Then Goode stepped up and slammed over the conversion to put his side even closer at Gloucester Rugby 22 – 20 Leicester Tigers.

With a mere twelve minutes left to play what had been a stroll in the park an hour earlier had somehow become an ascent of Everest for Gloucester as Goode slotted a penalty to put Leicester ahead for the very first time in the match at Gloucester Rugby 22 – 23 Leicester Tigers; but as we all know, the only time in a rugby match you really need to be in the lead is when the final whistle is blown.

Then Walker dropped a goal. We turned over possession and Willie was way back on the right hand touchline when he unleashed his right footed attempt. It wobbled in the air and needed a bit of assistance as it ricocheted off the right hand post but the ref's hand went up and so did Gloucester voices.

We were back in the lead at Gloucester Rugby 25 – 23 Leicester Tigers with seconds to go and Leicester had possession. We all knew what was going to be attempted but it still had to be executed.

Talk about "Eye of the Tiger"... thirty Leicester Tigers' eyes were fixed on our goalposts and the coldest, most calculating pair of them all belonged to Andy Goode. Expressionless yet with a depth of concentration that non-kickers can only dream of, he bided his time while his team maintained possession and took the ball ever closer to the Gloucester line. When he judged himself to be within his distance they gave him possession and the kick was taken.

The scene was like a slow-motion shot from an American cult sports-comedy film. Kingsholm was silent. So slowly the ball arced towards the posts that you ought to have believed that it could never travel that far that slowly; but all the time you knew it would. Kingsholm was still silent.

The ball reached the top of its trajectory and you could see that it was accurate but would it have the legs? Kingsholm remained silent. The ball bisected the posts, the referee signified the score and Kingsholm was no longer silent.

For the first time an away team had won a play off match and Sod's Law dictated that it would be against Gloucester at Kingsholm. Once more Leicester had rained on our bonfire, forcing a disappointing and unsatisfactory end to our season...

GLOUCESTER RUGBY	LEICESTER TIGERS
Try: S-Daniel	**Try:** Mauger, Tuilagi
Conversion: Lamb	**Conversion:** Goode (2)
Penalty Goal: Lamb (5)	**Penalty Goal:** Goode (3)

OTHER SEMI FINAL RESULT
London Wasps 21 – 10 Bath Rugby

THE LONG AND THE SHORT...

LE BON, LA BRUTE ET LE TRUAND...

GLOUCESTER A

SOUTHERN CONFERENCE

Monday 8 October 2007
Kick off 7.30pm Imber Court
Harlequins A 59 – 0 Gloucester A

Monday 5 November 2007
Kick off 7.30pm Kingsholm
Gloucester A 28 - 42 Bath United

Try: J Forster, D Oselton (2), O Winterbottom
Conversion: M Davies
Penalty Goal: M Davies (2)

Monday 26 November 20
Kick off 7.30pm Clifton RFC
Bristol United 29 - 8 Gloucester A

Try: D Oselton
Penalty Goal: M Davies

Monday 7 January 2008
Kick off 7.15pm Cleve RFC
Bath United 56 - 14 Gloucester A

Try: D Gordon (2)
Conversion: M Davies (2)

Monday 14 January 2008
Kick off 7.30pm Billesley Common
London Wasps 12 - 63 Gloucester A

Try: M Davies, H Trinder
Conversion: M Davies

Monday 3 March 2008
Kingsholm
Gloucester A - Bristol United
POSTPONED

Monday 10 March 2008
The Avenue
London Irish – Gloucester A
POSTPONED

Monday 17 March 2008
Billesley Common
Harlequins – Gloucester A
POSTPONED

Monday 24 March 2008
kick off 7.30pm Woolam Playing Field
Saracens 48 - 40 Gloucester A

Try: Adams (2), Bailey, Pendlebury, Prendergast
Conversion: Davies (3)
Penalty goal: Davies (3)

Monday 31 Mar 2008
Billesley Common
London Irish – Gloucester A
POSTPONED

Monday 7 Apr 2008
Billesley Common
Saracens – Gloucester A
POSTPONED

Monday 14 April 2008
Dry Leas
London Wasps – Gloucester A
POSTPONED

This match was postponed due to injury concerns. As no alternative dates were available London Wasps were awarded the win with a 20 - 0 scoreline, including a try bonus point (Guinness 'A' League rules 06/07).

GUINNESS A LEAGUE
Southern Conference

Pos	Team	Played	W	D	L	F	A	TF	TA	TB	LB	P
1	Harlequins	10	7	0	3	338	187	46	24	4	2	34
2	Saracens	10	6	0	4	357	263	51	36	7	3	34
3	L Wasps	7	6	0	1	291	120	42	15	5	1	30
4	Bristol United	10	5	0	5	236	262	33	37	4	0	24
5	London Irish	9	4	0	5	162	242	23	35	3	1	20
6	Bath United	10	3	0	7	213	328	30	48	3	3	18
7	Gloucester A	6	0	0	6	102	297	15	45	2	0	2

GUINNESS A LEAGUE
Northern Conference

Pos	Team	Played	W	D	L	F	A	TF	TA	TB	LB	P
1	Northampton	10	8	0	2	248	185	34	24	5	0	37
2	Newcastle F	10	7	0	3	268	241	35	31	4	9	32
3	Worcester	9	4	0	4	270	203	36	25	3	2	25
4	Leeds Car	10	4	0	6	220	263	23	34	2	2	20
5	Leicester T	10	4	0	6	270	226	35	25	2	0	18
6	Sale Sharks	9	1	0	8	111	269	14	38	1	3	8

GLOUCESTER ACADEMY

Gloucester Academy Senior Squad

Dave Blackwell

Freddie Burns

Adrian Duncan

Jonny May

Jed Hooper

Shaun Knight

Dave Lewis

Dan Norton

Jordi Pasqualin

Tristan Roberts

Charlie Simpson-Daniel

Yann Thomas

Guy Thompson

Henry Trinder

Dan Williams

Ollie Winterbottom

Danny Wright

Dave Blackwell

Freddie Burns

Adrian Duncan

Jed Hooper

Shaun Knight

Dave Lewis

Jonny May

Daniel Norton

Jordi Pasqualin

Tristan Roberts

Charlie S-Daniel

Yann Thomas

Guy Thompson

Henry Trinder

Dan Williams

Ollie Winterbottom

Danny Wright

MARK CORNWELL
The Gloucester A and Academy manager talks about his season

GLOUCESTER A

It has been a very difficult season for Gloucester A. Some of the participating clubs do not take it seriously – in fact at least three of them will not be participating next year - and it can sometimes be hard to raise a team when some of our Academy players are representing other clubs, which they have been entitled to do under RFU legislation this season.

The ruling was passed to ensure that Academy players get sufficient playing time. They are allowed to play for any other club.

The number of postponed matches was disappointing and as yet it is still uncertain whether an A league will be operated next season. Bath, Bristol and London Irish are definitely pulling out and they are all in the Southern Conference, where we play. Without them there would only be Gloucester, Harlequins, Saracens and Wasps. It is unlikely that a league of only four teams would run and so there is a question mark over the Southern Conference. An option would be to have a national A league but that would mean travelling up to Newcastle and Sale for Monday night kick offs and nobody is very keen on that.

I still think the A League will be run next season, but nobody knows what form it will take.

GLOUCESTER ACADEMY

As regards the Academy, our senior Academy has now increased in size to seventeen players for next season, with a couple leaving and ten new players coming on board. They have all been set up with one-year contracts. We now have some of the brightest young rugby talent in the country.

They are coming to Gloucester because we have created the sort of environment which young players want to join and be a part of. We are generating a reputation as a breeding ground for young talent and that is something we would like to work on and improve.

We have brought on senior squad players like Ryan Lamb, Nick Wood and Ollie Morgan. They stand testament to what we are trying to achieve here.

We are very excited about working with the new players. There is one name among the newcomers which is not unknown to Gloucester supporters. Scrum half Charlie Simpson-Daniel is the youngest of the Simpson-Daniel brothers. He has just finished his A levels at Sedburgh School.

Then we have fly half Freddie Burns. He joins us from Bath Academy and has already represented England at Under-18 level.

Shaun Knight is also an England Under-18 player. Shaun is a tighthead prop. His dad played hooker for Gloucester some years ago. Shaun is strong and uncompromising. A good scrummager.

Also in the front row is Shaun's England Under-18 team mate loosehead prop Yann Thomas who joins us from Bristol.

Between these two we have England Under-18 hooker Dave Blackwell.

Danny Wright is an England Under-18 lock. He joins us with the reputation of being more than useful in the lineout.

Jordi Pasqualin – a scrum half - is an ex-King's School pupil and was a member of the England Under-18 Conference a year early.
Jordi scored a try for Gloucester in the Middlesex Sevens last summer.

Winger Ollie Winterbottom also represented the England Under-18 Conference a year early.

Completing the intake are centre Jonny May, who joins from Hartpury College team.
Flyhalf Tristan Roberts, who has represented England Students and played a pivotal role in helping Cinderford achieve promotion to National Two this season.
And last, but not least openside Guy Thompson from the University of the West of England in Bristol.

Gloucester Academy is very lucky to have players of this quality to work with and we are all looking forward to the 2008 – 2009 season.

Mark was talking at the end of May 2008

In the same series
Hard Yards: Gloucester Rugby Yearbook 2006 – 2007

Please use a copy of the coupon below to order back copies of
Hard Yards : Gloucester Yearbook 2006 – 2007

or more copies of this edition direct from
Hard Yards Books
59 Dinglewell
Gloucester
GL3 3HP

---

lease send ...... copies of
Hard Yards: Gloucester Rugby Yearbook 2006 – 2007

@ £5.95 each

lease send ...... copies of
Hard Yards: Gloucester Rugby Yearbook 2007 – 2008
@ £7.95 each

include £2.50 post & packaging costs

enclose a cheque made payable to **Hard Yards Books** of the value
f £............ as payment in full

AME: ....

DDRESS: ....

....

OST CODE: ....

ease allow 28 days for delivery. Do not send cash.
